CONCILIUM

Religion in the Seventies

CONCILIUM

Concilium 127 (7/1979): Church Order

THE ROMAN CURIA AND THE COMMUNION OF CHURCHES

Edited by

Peter Huizing
and
Knut Walf

THE SEABURY PRESS / NEW YORK

1979
The Seabury Press, 815 Second Avenue, New York, N.Y. 10017
ISBN: 0-8164-0139-X   0-8164-2042-4 (pbk.)

T. & T. Clark Ltd., 36 George Street, Edinburgh EH2 2LQ
ISBN: 0-567-30007-2 (pbk.)

Library of Congress Catalog Card Number: 79-56600
Printed in the United States of America

CONTENTS

Part III
Projecting Collegial Institutions into the Future

Editorial

ON NOVEMBER 21 1970, Paul VI instituted an age limit for cardinals effective from January 1 1971. This had already been done for the diocesan bishops and the parish priests. This limit meant that those cardinals who were permanently connected with the Vatican were to put their office at the disposal of the pope out of their own free will in their seventy-fifth year. Their colleagues who administered a diocese outside Rome already were obliged to do this. All the duties of the cardinal's office were to be resigned in their eightieth year. They would then also be unable to participate in the conclave for the election of a pope.

As a reaction to this, Cardinal Ottaviani who had become eighty on October 29 1970, stated in an interview to the Roman daily *Il Messaggero,* that the pope had infringed canon law in taking this step. Ottaviani had too detailed a knowledge of canon law not to know that the legal status of cardinals regarding the election of a pope was unassailable even by the pope himself.

Lécuyer's contribution in this issue mentions that as recently as the middle of the previous century eminent canonists, such as Bouix, still wrote that the theory which held that the college of cardinals dated back to apostolistic times and which claimed that it was an institution of 'divine right' was not without grounds. Bouix himself, however, was of a different opinion. Alberigo's article mentions a speech which Ottaviani once gave on the occassion of Pope John XXIII's visit to the 'Highest Sacred Congregation of the Holy Office'—*Suprema Sacra Congregatio Sancti Officii.* Being the head of this first and highest organ of the curia, Ottaviani conveys the feelings of all the members of the curia in his speech when he talks about 'that unique and illustrious body'; 'a so illustrious and ancient institution that it seems to have its roots in the times of the apostles themselves'; 'yet so youthful in its ardent and fruitful industry that it appears to be born yesterday'. It seems as though there must have been a connection between his reference to the apostolic foundation of the early days of the curia and his later reproach of the pope to the effect that the latter had assailed the legal status of the cardinals. The theory which sees the medieval construction of the college of cardinals as an institution of 'divine right' has apparently cast its shadows far into the second half of our century; and Ottaviani is perhaps not its only upholder.

Although there is no doubt as to the contingent historical and positive canonical character of this college of cardinals and the Roman curia, its theological position is still not without ambiguity. This is especially apparent in the situation in which Paul VI left the curia by making the synod of bishops a competing advisory body to the pope.

The Roman curia is the complex of cardinal congregations, offices (*officia*), legal bodies, secretariats, and papal representatives outside the Vatican with which the pope administers the world Church. To this belong neither the curia of the Vicariate of Rome, the administrative body which the pope uses in his capacity as the bishop of the diocese of Rome, nor the staff who are at his disposal as the head of state of the Vatican City.

Although Paul VI allowed the members of the coucil of prelates to speak about the reorganisation of the curia, he made it plain that only he himself, and not the council or the college of bishops, had the right to take decisions concerning this issue. In an address to the Rota on September 21 1963, he characterised the curia as an organ which stood in direct contact with the pope and which observed strict obedience to him in his contribution to the universal mission. He confirmed that much reorganisation was necessary, but the curia itself would be able to establish and implement this.

In response to this, the Council expressed a few broadly formulated wishes. The reorganisation should meet the requirements of the various countries and rites. Above all it should consider the number, powers, mutual co-operation, and the working methods of the various departments of the curia. Its members, functionaries and advisors, and the papal representatives outside the Vatican should be recruited from as many different areas as possible, so that the central body of the Church would acquire a truly universal character. Bishops, especially diocesan bishops who can best convey the needs of all the different churches to the pope, should also be appointed as members of the curia. (*Christus Dominus,* nos. 9 and 10).

The pope decreed on August 6 1967 that seven diocesan bishops would be assigned to each congregation for a five-yearly period. They would be appointed on the recommendation of the head of the congregation after the latter has consulted the conference of bishops. Because of their obligation to live within their dioceses, these bishops would be able to attend only the yearly plenary meeting of their congregation in order to discuss the broad directives of its activities. Consequently they can only exercise a limited say.

The reorganisation of the curia which is based on the constitution 'For the rule of the universal Church' (*Regimini Ecclesiae universae*), dated August 15 1967, has accentuated its role as the executive body of the pope even more. This is not only because of the imposed age limit of its staff, but also because the heads, members and advisors of its departments are appointed for five years at a time, even though it is possible for them to be re-appointed. Moreover, a new pope must confirm all appointments within three months of his election. Also, cardinals who are the head of a department must resign their office at the death of a pope. Not to mention that there no longer exist any rights of promotion. The pope has in this way obtained a wider scope in the choice of his staff. The cardinal secretary of state calls together on a regular basis all the cardinals who are heads of a department in order to co-ordinate their duties and activities. This has in practice led to a situation in which all business reaches the pope via that secretariat. It has as a consequence developed into a miniature replica of the curia with various departments. By declaring all the congregations equal before the law, so that the congregation lost its priority on doctrinal grounds, the pope has been able to obtain a firmer grip on the course of things through the centralisation of his secretariat.

The curia has been noticeably extended and strengthened under the rule of Paul VI. The number of staff has risen from 1,322 in 1961 to 3,146 in 1977. The higher posts and temporary functions, such as that of advisor, have become less Roman and more international. The share of the 'Third Worlds' in such positions has also increased. However, as was to be expected, the middle and lower ranking posts are predominantly Italian. The departments of the 'new curia' are the most extensively internationalised. These include the various commissions, the Council for the Laity, *Justitia et Pax,* and *Cor Unum* for the co-ordination of the institutions which concern themselves with aid and the developing countries. Sixty per cent of the senior staff is non-Italian and they were not previously members of the curia but are former diocesan bishops. The papal representations have also greatly increased in number, especially in Africa, Asia and Oceania where the staff is also of a more international mix (for more details see Giancarlo Zizola, *Quale Papa? Anilisi delle Strutture Elettorali e Governantive del Papato Romano,* Roma 1977, pp. 228-233).

The synod of bishops was instituted by Paul VI on September 15 1965, during the fourth session of Vatican II (see *Apostolica Sollicitudo;* also revised regulation of the synod June 24 1969). The composition of the synod varies according to whether a general, special, or extraordinary meeting has been called. A general meeting deals with topics pertinent to the Church as a whole, which requires the consultation of the world episcopacy. The participants in this meeting are: the patriarchs; the archbishops; the bishops elected by the bishop conferences—1, 2, 3 or 4 may be sent by a conference, depending on whether the membership of the conference is less than 25, between 25 and 50, between 50 and 100, or more than 100 respectively; 10 male religious as representatives of the priestly orders and congregations, chosen by the Union of General Superiors; together with the cardinals who are at the head of a department in the curia. An extraordinary meeting deals with similar topics but which require a speedy decision. The presidents of the conferences of bishops rather than elected bishops, and 3 rather than 10 religious attend this meeting. A special meeting is held in order to deal with matters which are of importance only to particular areas. Only members from those areas and the cardinals of the curia who head the department which deals with that area attend. The pope has the power to appoint other bishops, priests and religious as members of a meeting of the synod, provided their number does not exceed fifteen per cent of the ordinary membership.

The synod is a permanent institution with periodical meetings every two or three years. The members are elected for one such meeting only. It has a permanent secretariat. It is not a department of the curia and stands under the direct authority of the pope. He has the exclusive right to call a meeting, determine its location, confirm the choice of members, draw up the topics for discussion, and the agenda. He is able to preside over the synod—either personally or by proxy—relocate it, cancel or shorten it, and appoint its general secretary and a few other officials. And finally, he has to take the decisions of the synod in consideration.

The synod can act only in an informative or advisory capacity to the pope, unless he specifically authorises it to take decisions on matters of concern. However, such decisions are not put into force until the pope has confirmed them. If the papacy falls vacant and a meeting of the synod has been convened, the meeting is cancelled until the new pope can take a decision on its fate.

The pope and the Roman curia. The commission for the revision of canon law has adopted canon 7 without change: '*Apostolic See* or *Holy See* shall be understood to mean not only the pope, but also the departments of the curia and other institutions through which the pope is wont to deal with matters of the universal Church, unless the context inidicates otherwise.' This poses the question of whether, and to what extent, the curia is part of the papal government.

Benedict XV stipulated at the very introduction of the code of canon law in 1917, that the organs of the curia would have no legislative powers but could give instructions only for the execution of the exclusively papal legislation. His successors have only formally stuck to this principle. No organ of the curia has ever published a document with the heading 'canon law'. In practice, however, they have allowed the departments to exercise a certain amount of legislative power. For instance, the legislation concerning married priests was promulgated by the congregation for the doctrine of faith. But even so, the dependence of the congregations on the legislative powers of the pope is maintained by standards laid down in the constitution *Regimini*: 'The first principle to be observed—*hoc in primis solemne sit*—by all departments of the curia is that no important or extraordinary matters may be dealt with without prior notification of the pope by the heads of departments. Moreover, the pope must give his approval to any conclusion reached before it comes into force. This excludes issues concerning which the heads of departments have been given full powers by the pope; it also excludes legal judgments of the Holy Roman Rota and the Apostolic Signatura'. No department of the curia ever issues any binding conclusions without the express mention of papal approval.

It has been asked whether the inclusion of the pope and the curia under the one title of the 'Holy' or 'Apostolic See' is a theological issue or simply a canonical construction.

This apparent identification creates no problems if regarded as a canonical construction. The canon law often mentions 'matters reserved for the Holy See', 'appeal to the Holy See' etc., without specifying all the time whether the pope himself or a department of his curia is being referred to. The relationship between the curia and the pope and the division of labour between the various departments is described for all cases in a general chapter which is separate from all the others and which at the moment can be found in the constitution *Regimini*. The term 'Holy See' is then used in all cases to refer to the legal structure described in that chapter.

On the other hand, the possibility of this terminology having a theological implication does raise problems. To begin with, it has become common usage to reserve the qualifying adjectives *holy* and *apostolic* for the bishop's see of Rome alone. However, this is not correct. Vatican II improved upon the phrase 'Peter and the apostles' by changing it into 'Peter and the other apostles' on the suggestion of Cardinal Alfrink. Had it been entirely consistent, then it should have changed 'the apostolic see of Rome and the other bishops' sees' into 'the see of Rome and the other apostolic bishops' sees'. One may easily say: 'It is only a way of speaking, but this way of speaking no longer corresponds to the view Vatican II takes of the apostolic college of bishops, including the "See of Rome"'.

But what about such qualifications as the 'Holy Congregations', the 'Holy Roman Rota', and the 'Apostolic Signatura'? That this kind of qualification is becoming obsolete as a manner of speech is borne out by the fact that the new style departments of the curia, the secretariats and even the synod of bishops do not use it. Not to say that their use in such cases would be dubious from a theological point of view, since it would seem as though the curia were hiding itself behind a cloak of papal authority were it to assume such qualifying adjectives. It goes without saying that the pope needs a staff to help him with the task of the universal mission. But only he himself and no one else can deal with the Church through papal authority. The theological 'sacral' character of the papal office rests on the sacramental character of his ordination as a bishop. It is not possible to delegate this sacramental character of the papal authority to a functionary whose authority ultimately rests upon an administrative appointment. Nor is it possible to bestow this authority on an institution, the existence and power of which depends upon administrative structures and appointments.

It seems, therefore, that on theological grounds it is very necessary to change terminology which no longer represents present-day views. It also seems that the regulation which states that the departments of the curia are not allowed to take any decisions other than those concerning issues of a routine nature, is not simply a purely canonical regulation.

Synod of bishops and the pope. The document *Apostolica Sollicitudo* gives the following reasons for the existence of the synod of bishops which it established: strengthening of the bonds between the pope and the bishops; a clearer and more direct participation by the bishops in the papal care of the world Church; direct and accurate information concerning the life and works of the various churches; facilitation of the unity of the college of bishops, especially in such essential matters as the life and doctrine of the Church.

On September 30 1971, during the first session of the synod of bishops, Paul VI declared that the bond of faith, love and pastoral care between the papal office and the episcopacy and between bishops and religious orders and congregations needed strengthening. Moreover, he said that the first two aims of this new organ of the pastoral office were the preservation of unity and community within the hierarchy and the giving of full support and advice to the pope. He also added that the synod did not have the authority of an ecumenical council because it had neither the correct composition nor the appropriate tasks. Nevertheless, it did have something of the air of such a council. The bishops represent the basis of unity of the churches, just as the pope is the basis of the Church of Rome, the Church as a whole, the episcopacy and all the religious. They represent the bishops' conferences who elect them. They depict the hierarchy of the Catholic Church, which in itself represents the only, highest and invisible head of the Church. The bishops also represent the Christian people, not so much as delegates, but as the representatives of Christ to these people.

The pope wishes only to listen during a meeting, in order to encourage all to give their free opinion. This is an eloquent exposition of his role in the synod. He participates but is not a member. This is comparable to the position of a bishop in his diocesan synod: he is the only one who takes the decisions which are legally independent of the propositions and wishes of the synod. Nevertheless, the pope quoted *Lumen gentium,* n. 22, when opening the extraordinary meeting of October 11 1969: 'Just as, by the Lord's will, St Peter and the other apostles constituted one apostolic college, so in a similar way the Roman Pontiff as the successor of Peter, and the bishops as the successors of the apostles are joined together.' He added to this that he had promoted this bond of brotherhood by instituting the synod of bishops. However, this synod is not a realisation of the brotherhood mentioned in the *Lumen gentium,* but a body like the curia in service to the personal primacy of the pope, created by himself. It does not represent the world episcopacy based on the sacramental mission received when becoming a bishop. Incidentally, Paul VI has repeatedly stated that the synod was open to further canonical developments as a human institution.

College of bishops and college of cardinals. Paul VI extended the membership of the college of cardinals to include nearly all the chairmen of the bishops' conferences and the leading figures of the various churches, including the more docile theologians. Preference was given to men from the Third World. In 1977 the membership comprised men from 53 different countries including 12 Africans and 9 Asians (Zizola, op. cit., pp. 178-181).

Cardinal Pellegrino, the Archbishop of Turin, published his proposal to make up the college of cardinals out of chairmen of the conferences of bishops for the duration of their office in September 1965. The pope would also be able to appoint additional cardinals. This proposal won the approval of a number of bishops both in and outside Italy. Pope Montini declared on June 28 1967, during the ceremony of the conferring of the red hats on the newly appointed cardinals that he had no reason to change his predecessors' system of appointments to the college of cardinals. If he were to do this, then the election of the pope would be subject to all sorts of dangerous influences. This was especially the case, since the calls for change would imply that the corps of cardinals was no longer a fully qualified and stable body protected from unacceptable interference. However, later on he did consider whether the chairmen of the bishops conferences should be included in the college of cardinal bishops for the purpose of the election of the pope. Nevertheless, he never actually implemented this idea. His most important reason for this seems to have been that the bishop of Rome needs to be chosen by the Church of Rome of which the cardinals are considered to be representatives, even if in name only.

More consternation was caused by an interview given by Cardinal Suenens to *Informations Catholiques Internationales* on May 15 1969. According to him, all the friction in the Church between the 'centre'— Rome—and the 'periphery'—the 'rest' of the Church—is caused by two conflicting views of the Church. On the one hand there is the structure which radiates from the 'centre' to the subordinate 'periphery', whilst on the other hand there is a framework of independent, localised churches which are linked to the Church of Rome, the centre of all unity. The first view obviously tends towards a centralised, juridical, bureaucratic and static unit. The second view envisages a more open structure with many rich varieties, rather than the few marginal differences allowed under the present system. These varieties would affect all areas of spirituality, liturgy, canon law, pastoral matters, etc. The first view tends to an isolation of the pope and his curia, whilst the other would produce a more open working relationship between the bishop of Rome and the college of bishops whose head he is. Bishops and even conferences of bishops are often prevented from carrying out decisions they have reached after deliberation with their clergy and their people simply because of an inflexible wielding of the law by the curia. Cardinals are selected according to criteria which nobody knows and which are not open to discussion. The Church should reflect more adequately her diversity at large in the membership of this college. This includes taking the age of the members into consideration. Concerning the ecclesiastical function of the papal representatives, why should there be papal inspectors at the bishops' courts if the synod of bishops has really established a direct means of communication and a brotherly relationship between the bishops and the pope? The papacy which possesses a unique and inalienable charisma of community would be freer to develop its world mission if it were to be liberated from a too centralised structure.

Paul VI always expressed feelings of humility and sincere objectivity when evaluating a criticism. He also showed great trust in the person who delivered such comments. Yet cardinals Daniélou, Felici, Tisserant and Villot, and head of the Vatican press bureau took up a strong position against Suenens in the *L'Osservatore Romano* of June 29 1969. The pope himself rebuked the general chapter of the Paulians who had published the interview in their newspaper *Famiglia Christiana*. By way of a reply to this, the newspaper staged a 'counter-interview' with Daniélou. On June 24 1969, just before the synod of bishops, the pope decreed a new regulation to reinforce the point that matters concerning the Roman curia fall entirely within his competence. Amongst those who expressed agreement with Suenens were Cardinals Alfrink and Pellegrino. The notoriously outspoken Monseignor Elias Zoghbi wondered whether we would have to wait for a new council of prelates to effect the change from an advisory Church to a brotherly Church.

The synod of bishops of 1974 also brought out the conflict between the view of the Church as a brotherly community of churches and the view of the Church as an organisation governed from the hierarchal top downwards. The frank comments of the churches from Africa, Asia and Latin America in particular were a great revelation. Seven out of the twelve 'smaller (linguistic) groups' expressed a positive opinion concerning the autonomy of the local churches. It was insisted that the decree concerning the pastoral duty of the bishops should be put into practice. This would mean that the various cultures within the Church would be able to express the multifarious forms of their own liturgy, theology and catechism. They also pressed for a discussion between Rome and the local churches. Rome cannot judge all local details, instead it must just listen and guide. It must act as the supreme authority only in fundamental and universal ecclesiastical matters. This opinion was supported by the majority of the conferences of bishops. Paul VI replied rather guardedly in his concluding speech. The papacy must not limit itself to just extraordinary situations. He also did not consider it safe to speak about theologies being as numerous and different as there are different continents and cultures. What is contained in the faith is either universally Catholic, or not Catholic at all.

Expectations. In this issue we have attempted to look at the theme 'Roman Curia and the Community of the Churches'. We have tried to consider this from a variety of standpoints. The first section of the issue presents a theological evaluation of the position of the curia. In it we have tried to give a treatment of the problem whether the curia as a body at the service to the pope can in fact be of service to the bond between the churches and the Church of Rome. A second section attempts to give an analysis of the functions of the different departments of the curia and presents some examples of existing relations between local churches and the curia. A third section tries to shed some light on a few possible developments.

In his very first speech, Pope John Paul II has raised hopes that he will continue to develop the solidarity and brotherly spirit of the college of bishops, the conferences of bishops and especially the synod of bishops. It should be realised that this has already been partially achieved in some local synods. It seems very likely that the view of Vatican II which regards the college of bishops as the leadership of the Church based on the apostolic succession and the sacramentally consecrated mission will determine the future central structures of the Church.

PETER HUIZING
KNUT WALF

(Translated by H. W. Hellinga)

Part I

Fundamental Subjects

Joseph Lécuyer

The Place of the
Roman Curia in Theology

TO CRITICISE or attack an institution is always both dangerous and attractive. It is dangerous because one is always tempted to be guided by personal motivations which throw doubts on one's objectivity. It is attractive because it gives one the feeling that in criticising or attacking one plays the judge of the institution, and this produces the subtle satisfaction of sitting in judgement on those that are part of the institution. But, as Han Urs von Balthasar put it, 'the only models of genuine protest are the saints'.[1] Such protest becomes a particularly delicate matter when it is aimed at an institution like the Roman curia, because, however one goes about it, one always appears to criticise the pope himself beyond the curia. Cardinal Lercaro put it very clearly during Vatican II: the Roman curia is an instrument of the papacy, and, in the end, only the pope is responsible for it to such an extent that nobody, not even the Council, is really competent to query it.[2] One cannot treat it as a body which is directly at the service of all the churches. It is only at the service of the pope himself so that he can carry out his absolutely unique and incommunicable function as supreme pastor, and the centre of the whole ecclesiastical community.[3] So, to criticise the curia is to criticise the instrument through which the pope has decided to fulfil in a normal way his mission as 'the servant of the servants of God'.

But, obviously, this does not mean that we cannot point out the flaws in such an institution. Both John XXIII and Paul VI asked the Council Fathers to tell them what they thought about the reform of the curia.[4] Although a large number of bishops stressed the value of this body, there were many suggestions about an improvement in the services it rendered.[5] In any case, no one reasonably acquainted with the curia today

3

would deny the great qualities, the competence, the dedication, the disinterestedness[6] or the ability of many of its members.[7] There are nevertheless also shortcomings which all admit[8] and among the first to denounce them are some members of the curia itself.[9] One of them, who later became a cardinal, wrote in 1970: 'The Church remains human in its members. Wherever man is found, one finds his limitations, his faults, and probably his sin. His supernatural mission is only worked out through structures that are imperfect and must be improved upon. And so it is with the curia, and even particularly with the curia where man is more easily tempted to power, showing-off, and what is called "triumphalism".'[10]

History shows that the Roman curia has not always been able to resist this temptation. It is easy to draw up a list of past abuses, even if many facts can be explained, if not justified, by the cultural and political context of the various periods.[11] One has only to think of the protests made by St Hildegard, St Brigit, St Catherine and others about the behaviour of the curia to understand that such criticisms are not necessarily without foundation.

For the moment we will concentrate only on a very limited aspect of this problem, the one which directly concerns theology: what kind of theological link is there between the Roman curia and the pope himself? Can one speak of the curia as 'sharing' in the mission and authority of the pope, and, if so, in what sense, and within what limits? I shall try to peg down a few relevant factors some of which seem in any case already generally accepted.

1. IS THE CURIA AN INSTITUTION OF DIVINE ORIGIN?

Nowadays nobody would uphold the idea that the curia was directly instituted by Christ. But in the past this was not always the case, at least in so far as the college of cardinals is concerned. As recently as the middle of the last century the canonist Bouix did indeed reject the divine institution of the cardinalate but only after qualifying this opinion as 'licit' and probable, after reviewing a long series of arguments brought up by the opposition.[12] In the wake of many others G. Alberigo produced a study in depth of this way of thinking and what follows is an outline of his thought.[13] First of all, it has to be pointed out that the question did not originally arise as centred on the 'curia' since it seems that the word was not used before the twelfth century. Gerhoh of Reichersberg (d. 1169) still protested against the introduction of this term.[14] The issue centred on the 'Ecclesia Romana'. This 'Ecclesia' was not identified with the pope but comprised also the college of cardinals. It was asserted that the powers of this church came without doubt from God Himself in so far as this church was the 'caput Ecclesiae' (the head of the Church at large). Peter Damian maintained that the primacy of this church was of divine origin: the cardinal-bishops share in the power of Peter's successor and, with him, hold the 'keys' of the Church. In other words, by the end of the twelfth century it was maintained that the cardinals shared in the pope's 'plenitudo potestatis' over the whole Church, while the rest of the bishops were only called 'in partem sollicitudinis'.[15]

There is little point in listing numerous other texts which support this idea, but it is worth mentioning the attempt made to provide the divine origin of the college of curial cardinals with a scriptural foundation. This line of argument maintained that the cardinals were to the pope what the seventy elders, designated by God (see Numbers 11), were to Moses,[16] or what the levitical priests mentioned in Deut. 17:8-11 were to the judge in office. Innocent III explained this text as meaning that the cardinals were the pope's coadjutors 'by levitical law'.[17] The pope is the stone whose seven eyes are the cardinals; he is the golden lamp-stand of which the seven lamps represent the cardinals—all according to Zechariah 3:9 and 4:2.[18] What seems even more astonishing is the wide-spread assertion that, by Christ's institution, the successors of the apostles are the cardinals grouped round the pope as the eleven were grouped round St Peter.[19]

These theories were particularly popular at the time of the conflict between Boniface VIII and Philip the Fair, and of the western schism.[20] This led to support for Peter Damian's idea that the Roman cardinals were superior to the patriarchs and bishops. As the canon lawyer, Henry of Suse (Hostiensis), put it: they are one with the pope and with him judge anything that concerns the Church.[21]

Today, particularly after Vatican II, such a stance looks rather out of date. And yet, as has been pointed out before, even in the last century Bouix was still afraid of being too outspoken in favour of the opposite point of view. It is even more astonishing to see certain recent authors take up a position close to those medieval supporters of the curia and uphold the priveleges of the cardinals as rights that cannot be queried.[22] But already since the Middle Ages there were those who boldly challenged these claims that the cardinalate (and, by implication, the Roman curia) was of divine origin. In spite of some ambiguity here and there, St Bernard stated plainly that the cardinals had no more power than the pope thought good to give them; and especially those cardinals who were not even bishops could not possibly have more power than the bishops of the whole world, as they pretended to have.[23]

For the first half of the fourteenth century, William of Ockham deserves particular mention. He insists that the cardinalate is nothing but a purely human institution created by the pope of his own will. They have no divine or apostolic origin whatever, and the 'college' of archbishops and bishops is above (*eminentius*) that of the cardinals.[24] During the same period the French canon lawyer Jean Le Moyne showed that he did not object to the honours bestowed on the cardinals but absolutely refused to recognise any divine or apostolic origin of the cardinalate. If the pope wished to consult his cardinals, that was fair enough, because he had to set an example of prudence in reaching his decisions.[25]

It is clear that this is the line taken by Vatican II: 'divine institution' is something which can only be applied to the college of bishops headed by the pope. This is the college which succeeded to that of the apostles headed by Peter.

2. DO CARDINALS SHARE IN PAPAL INFALLIBILITY?

The matter of sharing the papal privileges, particularly that of infallibility in doctrine as defined by Vatican I, must be argued on the same lines as the previous point.

On July 11 1870, Msgr. Vincent Gasser, who reported on behalf of the Commission on Faith, made a very important speech before the actual definition took place. In it he made it perfectly clear that this papal prerogative was 'personal' in the real sense; it was not seen as the privilege of an abstract papacy, but as belonging to the pope who was actually responsible at such a moment in time.[26]

Yet here, too, there was a tendency to extend this infallibility to the cardinals, if not to the whole curia. This view, of course, follows logically from the idea that the cardinals succeeded the apostolic college united with St Peter. One can understand that at the time of the western schism there were some who thought that, *via* this cardinalitial infallibility, they could get out of the doctrinal deadlock. This was, for instance, the case with St Vincent Ferrier.[27] But even at that time there were many who objected to this way of thinking. Here Alberigo mentions the German theologians Konrad von Gelnhausen and Heinrich Haynbuch von Langenstein,[28] whose reasoning nevertheless was not faultless since they refused infallibility even to the magisterium of the successors to the apostles and the pope. They maintained that only the whole body of the faithful (*universitas fidelium*) could claim these promises of infallibility.

The French Benedictine Pierre Bohier, who became bishop of Orvieto, tackled this issue in a way which seems more satisfactory. According to him the only real successors to the apostles are the bishops and the universal Church is present in any of the individual churches over which the bishops preside. There is no divine institution of cardinals and they are not the successors of the apostles. As in the other individual churches, so in Rome they can only be the counsellors and assistants of their local bishop.[29] This kind of ecclesiology did perhaps not stress as much as it could the particular magisterial function of the pope, but at least it re-affirmed the traditional conception of the magisterium of the bishops which seemed to be crushed under the weight of the cardinalate and, by implication, the curia.

In 1859, when controversies raged about infallibility and led to its definition by Vatican I, the canon lawyer Bouix clearly formulated the position which was ultimately adopted by the Council: 'The privilege of infallibility (*inerrantiae*) granted by God to the bishop of Rome is exclusively personal; the Sovereign Pontiff can in no way share this prerogative with anyone else'.[30] The meaning of 'personal' differs from the one given to this adjective in the course of the debates of Vatican I, particularly as a result of Cardinal Guidi's intervention.[31] Yet Bouix's thought is clear enough in so far as the pope's relation to the curia is concerned. In no way can the curia share in the privilege of infallibility, and the pope himself cannot share this privilege with others or delegate it.

In actual fact, if we want to be more accurate and adopt the terminology of Vatican I, it is not so much the 'person' of the pope who is infallible as his *magisterium*. The curia can and must cooperate in the exercise of this papal function. Here again Msgr. Gasser put it very clearly: 'We do not deny in any way that the Church must contribute to an infallibility which is granted to the pope in no sense as inspiration or revelation but simply on the grounds of divine assistance. This is why the pope is bound, in view of his function and the importance of the issue at stake, to make use of any opportune means in order to find out and express the truth as accurately as possible. And this is why we have the Councils and the consultations with bishops, cardinals, theologians. . . .'[32] This obviously is the aspect of the question which lends weight to the curia. The services it renders must on no account ignore the whole of the Church, particularly the bishops. In fact, its best contribution lies precisely in this listening to and consulting the faith of the whole infallible Church: 'The deposit of the revelation was entrusted to the universal Church. So its preservation, interpretation and the pursuit of its actual meaning is everybody's business under the guidance of Peter. . . . This is why Peter must constantly listen and learn, and never go his own way.'[33]

As soon as the curia becomes self-centred, thinks that it is infallible and can ignore what all the other faithful feel or think, it will be unfaithful to the Spirit and serve the pope in the worst possible way by isolating him and cutting his indispensable contact with the whole People of God. Yet, it is this People of God which 'by the sense of faith, aroused and sustained by the Spirit of truth clings without fail to the faith once delivered to the saints, penetrates it more deeply by accurate insights, and applies it more thoroughly to life' (*Lumen Gentium,* 12).

3. THE CURIA AS AN INSTRUMENT OF GOVERNMENT

While the pope cannot share his *infallible* magisterium with others, he can share or delegate some of his authority in the area of government and canonical discipline. The curia obviously has this kind of power. According to canonists the curia has a jurisdiction which is '*ordinary* as well as *vicarious* and by implication covers the whole Church. . . . All these juridical bodies act in the name and by the authority of the Sovereign Pontiff. Their competence which, as has been said, extends to the whole Church and demands the obedience of all the faithful, is exclusive within the limits set to each individual body.'[34] Theologically there is no way of maintaining that the Roman Congregations are part of the *constitution* of the Church because this 'constitution' has fundamentally been laid down by Christ, its founder. All the same Christ certainly gave Peter the task of 'shepherding' the whole flock and 'to support his brethren', and so, by implication, he bestowed upon him the right and the duty to use the means necessary to fulfil this task. The curia is one of those means, 'the instrumental body which the Roman Pontiff uses to exercise the supreme power over the whole Church which he possesses because of Christ's own institution'.[35]

The powers of the curia are totally subject to the pope and it has no authority beyond what he grants it. While the bishops have their functions bestowed upon them by the very fact of their consecration, even if the exercise of these functions may be subject to certain conditions (see *Lumen Gentium,* 21), those of the curia are always 'vicarious', totally dependent on the pope. The constitution *Regimini Ecclesiae Universae* again stresses that 'all decisions must have the pope's approval'.[36] Whether this approval is given *in forma communi* or *in forma specifica* is of little theological significance. As long as the curia does not exceed the competence it has been granted, it conveys the pope's intent. One can hardly object that this view subjects the college of bishops to the curia, for neither the curia nor the college of bishops can be thought of without the pope. It is ultimately the pope as the head of the college of bishops who is responsible for the decisions of the curia.

It is hardly surprising that members of the curia have from time to time ill-used or abused their power. Anyone invested with authority, even at the lowest level, may be tempted to lord it over others instead of serving them (see Luke 22:25-26). One may well judge that the ambitions of the curia have been for a large part responsible for the excessive centralisation which, with so many other misapprehensions, led to the schism of the east. St Bernard did not mince his words when he attacked the ostentatiousness and worldly ambition of the papal court. But he also protested against the vast increase of appeals and the centralisation which reduced the role of the bishops to practically nothing, which runs counter to Christ's will: 'If you cut off the finger of a hand and attach it to the head . . . you create a monster. It is the same if, in the mystical body of Jesus Christ, you arrange the members in a way different from his.'[37]

Fundamentally it is a matter of choosing between two concepts of the Church: a pontifical monarchy or a communion. The curia, seen as the *papal court,* will obviously always be tempted to favour the first concept. Would it be possible to hope for a radical change, like the one suggested by some bishops before and during Vatican II? In this perspective the curia would become a consultative and executive body at the service, not only of the pope, but of a decision-taking body consisting of the pope and the cardinals together with a gathering of bishops elected from the whole Church.[38] This involves the whole issue of whether the supreme power should be exercised personally or collegially. But this issue is outside our theme.

Yet, even if we accept that the setting up of such a central collegial body would be possible, would it really change the character of the Roman curia? For even in this hypothesis the pope would obviously retain the absolutely special function which is his and which he could not share with others. He could never accept the position where he would merely carry out the decisions taken by a central body, even if he presides over it. As Fr. Congar put it, 'he always retains the power to exercise his authority in a personal and independent way, and therefore without necessarily and formally having to consult other bishops'.[39] Such a function can never be accomplished for the good of the whole Church without the help of consultants and assistants. The pope will therefore always need to have with him some bodies which, in the words of John Paul I, 'make it possible for him to fulfil in a concrete way the apostolic service which he owes to the whole Church, and thus ensure the organic expression of legitimate autonomies in the context of that indispensable respect for the essential unity, not only of faith but also of discipline, for which Christ prayed on the eve of his passion'.[40]

This expression of the *legitimate authorities* and the *essential* unity of faith and discipline contains the two demands which the pope will always have to face, helped by the curia.

Translated by Theo L. Westow

Notes

1. Hans Urs von Balthasar *Der antirömische Affekt* (Freiburg i.B. 1974).
2. See *Acta Synodalia S.Conc. Vat. II,* vol. II, 4, p. 620.
3. Cereti and Sartori, in their art. 'The Curia at the service of a renewed papacy' in *Concilium* 108 (1975) still show this confusion.
4. See Paul VI's Allocution at the second session (*Act. Ap. Sed.,* 55, 1963, pp. 849-850).
5. See I. Gordon, 'De Curia Romana renovata' in *Periodica de re Morali et Liturgica* 58 (1969) pp. 59-116.
6. Paul VI, Allocution of 21.9.1963 (*Act. Ap. Sed.* 55, 1963).
7. H. Urs von Balthasar, op. cit. pp. 42-43.
8. *Ibid.,* pp. 47; 110; 271-272 and 332.
9. See G. M. Garrone *L'Eglise* (Paris 1972) pp. 133-141.
10. P. Palazzini in N. del Re *La Curia Romana* (3rd ed., Rome 1970) p. xiv.
11. See the numerous facts gathered by F. Ieist in his *Der Gefangene des Vatikans* (Munich 1971).
12. D. Bouix *Tractatus de Curia Romana* (Paris 1859) pp. 50-51.
13. G. Alberigo *Cardinalato e Collegialità* (Florence 1969).
14. Introduction to his *Commentary on Ps. 64, P.L.* 194, cc. 9-10.
15. See Alberigo, op. cit., pp. 22f., 36-42, 44-45, 69-72.
16. Thus St Bernard, Pierre d'Ailly, Torquemada, and others. See Alberigo op. cit. p. 72.
17. *Epist. V,* 128 (*P.L.* 214, cc. 1132-1133). This text found its way into the *Corpus Iuris Canonici* (ed. Friedberg, 2, 716).
18. St Peter Damian *De Dignitate Romanae Ecclesiae et Episcopali Studio Disciplina* (*P.L.* 144, cc. 253-259).
19. See Alberigo op. cit. pp. 86-93.
20. *Ibid.* pp. 117f. and 159f.
21. *Ibid.* pp. 36-42 and 97-105.
22. For instance R. Raffalt *Wohin steuert der Vatikan?* (Munich 1973), p. 113.
23. *De Consideratione,* L. IV, IV, 9 and L. IV, V, 16.
24. See Alberigo op. cit. p. 141.
25. *Ibid.* pp. 145f.—This theory of the divine right of the cardinalate was not abandoned finally till the second half of the sixteenth century. See G. Alberigo *Lo Sviluppo Della Dottrina sui Poteri Nella Chiesa Universale* (Rome 1964) pp. 106f.
26. Mansi *S. Conc. Collectio* vol. 52, pp. 1212-1213.
27. See Alberigo *Cardinalato* etc. (see note 13) pp. 171f.
28. *Ibid.* pp. 168-182.
29. See D. Prerovsky 'Pietro Bohier vescovo, riformatore all' inizio dello scisma d'Occidente' in *Salesianum* 28 (1966) pp. 495-517; see also *ibid.* pp. 626-671.
30. Bouix *Tractatus de Curia Romana* (Paris 1859) p. 475.
31. See J. P. Torrell 'L'infaillibilité pontificale est-elle un privelège "personnel"?' in *Rev. Sc. Phil. et Théol.* 45 (1961) pp. 229-245.
32. Mansi op. cit. vol. 52, p. 1213.
33. H. Urs von Balthasar, op. cit. p. 328.

34. N. del Re *La Curia Romana* (3rd ed., Rome 1970) p. 49.

35. *Const. Regimini Ecclesiae Universae (Acta Ap. Sed.* 59, 1967, p. 887). See also the Decree *Christus Dominus,* n. 9.

36. *Ibid.,* n. 136, p. 928.

37. See B. Jacqueline *Papauté et Épiscopat selon S. Bernard de Clairvaux* (Saint-Lô 1963) pp. 67f., 112-116 and 120. The quotation is from *De Consideratione* III, IV, 17 (*P.L.* 182, c. 768c).

38. For the antepreparatory period see *Acta et Documenta Conc. Oecumenici Vat. II,* Ser. I, vol. II/1, p. 511; vol. II/6, pp. 50-51; vol. III, p. 23. See also the amendments proposed in the *Schema De Episcopis (Acta Synodalia,* etc., vol. II, 1, pp. 921-922).

39. Y. Congar *Ministères et Communion Ecclésiale* (Paris 1971).

40. Allocution to the Cardinals, of August 30 1978 (*Acta Ap. Sed.* 70, 1978, p. 703).

Giuseppe Alberigo

Serving the
Communion of Churches

AN ANALYSIS of the Roman curia seen from the standpoint of pastoral service within the framework of an ecclesiology of communion among the churches, achieved under the presidency in charity of the Church of Rome and its bishop, proves to be a very difficult undertaking. In fact, unless one postulates an *a priori* suitability, outside the limitations of time and space, of the Roman curia to carry out all necessary functions in the Church, what clearly springs to view is the structural remoteness of the curia from considerations of a pastoral nature and those affecting communion, at least as we understand these today.

This impression requires verification, particularly from a historical viewpoint, since we are dealing with an institution several centuries old, and one that would like to claim even more remote historical origins for itself.[1] The opinion most generally accepted among historians would place the origins of the curia in the eleventh and twelfth centuries. But this general affirmation leaves two important questions unresolved. The first is that some of the curial offices can justly claim more remote origins; the second that since the twelfth century, the curia has not developed in a straight line, but has undergone major changes, which throw light on the real relationship between the curia itself and pastoral service to the communion of churches. Any account of the main historical phases of the Roman curia has to pay attention to this basic characteristic of its evolution, in which institutional continuity and innovation have continually followed one another.

12

1. ADMINISTRATIVE AND FINANCIAL FUNCTIONS

The last centuries of the first millennium testify to a certain number of people helping the bishop of Rome, more often in relation to the public functions they carried out in the civil order than in relation to the life of the whole Church. In this respect, the bishop of Rome shared his decision-making responsibility with the Roman synod—which met once a week—whereas the administrative or bureaucratic functions were far less regular and could be carried out by a very small number of people. Gradually, however, two centres were formed, called respectively the 'chancellery', which drew up documents relating to requests for benefices, and the 'camera', responsible for the collection of rents, tithes and taxes.[2] Both were technical offices, with very limited staffs and a number of executive functions which were strictly defined and seen as being of secondary importance. Real decisions affecting the juridical aspects of the Church were at this time taken by the Lateran synods. These two embryonic centres of a curial structure were clearly removed both from the decision-making process and from any pastoral involvement.

Centralisation of Juridical and Canonical Decisions

The Gregorian reform and the gradual shift of the area of the Latin communion of churches westward during the second half of the eleventh and throughout the twelfth centuries was characterised by a marked centralisation of the juridical and canonical decision-making bodies in Rome. The seat of these processes was still the Roman synod—as witness the great Lateran Councils of 1123, 1139, 1179 and 1215—to which the consistory, the cardinals under the presidency of the pope, was gradually affiliated. This centralisation, originally ordered because of the need to carry out the reforms, and therefore to ensure a majority of bishops favourable to the reforms over those opposed to them, still sowed some seeds of organic centralisation. There was a tendency to a certain canonical unification (the *Concordia discordantium canonum* of Gratian) and to a centralisation of decisions on matters of major importance—here the concept of *causae maiores* acquired its significance—such as election of bishops and relations with the political authorities. The need to make opportune decisions in a short space of time favoured the slipping-away of competence in these matters from the Roman synod to the consistory. Looking back on this historical development, we can now appreciate its importance as being ecclesiological and not merely institutional. In the synod, the bishop of Rome took decisions effectively in conjunction with the representatives of the other Latin churches; in the consistory, the pope had recourse to a restricted group of people in the formulation of decisions that from an ecclesiological viewpoint always remained personal ones. The Roman curia naturally felt the effects of this major procedural change: the original nuclei increased numerically and added a juridical structure to cope with appeals made to Rome against local decisions. This could not but have the effect of increasing the 'political' weight of these offices: evidence of this is provided by the fact that under Innocent III, at the end of the twelfth century, all documents emanating from the curia were henceforth subject to the exaction of a corresponding tax. This indicates the growing financial needs of the head of the Church, and therefore the ever-increasing importance of the office responsible for fulfilling these needs. This was of course a most significant innovation in the structure of the Church, which began to show a marked shift away from the concept of a communion of churches to that of a universal community. This brought about an expansion of the curial offices responsible for the administrative and financial aspects of this *sollicitudo omnium ecclesiarum*; nevertheless, these offices remained subordinate and removed from pastoral responsibility, comprising a very limited sector of the total activities of Rome.

2. CENTRALISATION IN THE LATE MIDDLE AGES

The Avignon period (1309-1376) is known to have brought about a further round of economic and financial centralisation, strengthening the tendencies that had developed in the twelfth century, which were also reinforced in the thirteenth by the centralised structure of the new mendicant orders. The consistory became increasingly the seat of important decisions relating to the universal Church, and correspondingly, though with a very compartmentalised correspondence, the papal curia widened the responsibility of its offices, gaining too much economic power in the process not to be widely envied. This new period in the life of the curia was marked by the building-up of a most extensive and far-reaching financial network, with its consequent availability of increasingly indispensable funds and concomitant ability to interfere in all sorts of decisions. Though still subordinate and outside pastoral concerns, it found a way round through its opportunities for interfering, occasioned by the practice of a tax payable for every papal document and the possibility of proliferating unnecessary documents (*commendams*, indulgences, etc.) for the sake of the revenue that could be derived.

Denunciation of this state of affairs and its distorting effect on ecclesiastical life was a constant theme, particularly from the fifteenth century on, reiterated both by solemn General Councils (Constance, Basle), and by the most prominent churchmen of the time, such as Nicholas of Cusa, to the extent that a whole series of popes was forced to plan reforms, though these were never carried out. Furthermore, the nepotism raging at the papal courts of the Renaissance further strengthened the curia, to which relatives of the pope were often appointed, at the same time as the popes began to rule in a more personal way, gradually freeing themselves from the approval of the consistory. The most characteristic act in this process was the appointment of the cardinal-nephew as the pope's right-hand man and head of his secretariat. The papacy suffered from the assimilation of absolutist ideas of secular monarchism and became increasingly intolerant of conditions (often nationalistic) imposed by the cardinals on the impartial family and broader policies of the various successors of Peter. The functions of co-ordination, compensation and synthesis which the consistory—albeit with some gaps and failures—had performed for several centuries went into a decline. The immediate causes of this were the apparent slowness with which the consistory functioned, the need to face up to particular problems of a specially serious and pressing nature (the anti-Protestant inquisition, interpretations of the Decrees of the Council of Trent), and the popes' demand for a free hand in political dealings with heads of State. But behind all these was the central fact of a new orientation, leading to the reaffirmation of the primacy of the pope in total independence and autonomy from any other ecclesiastical body. The papal office, subjected to radical criticism by the Protestants and to trenchant satire, seemed to prefer to answer these by an institutional and authoritarian re-statement of its position, rather than by running the risk of undertaking a charismatic renewal of its own image, as indeed many informed sectors of the Counter-reformation Church suggested it should.

The 'Sistine Reform'

It was left to the post-Tridentine papacy, acting in a framework of an already universalist and centralist ecclesiology, to bring about the most significant change in the whole history of the central government of the western Church. We know how Sixtus V, in 1588, without actually abolishing the consistory, defined its competence within a series of limited spheres, to each of which a group of cardinals was assigned, who were to prepare matters for the decision of the full session of the true and proper consistory. The Sistine reform, though few foresaw it,[3] was to have traumatic results. In fact, under the guise of a purely technical exercise in efficacity, it substantially restructured the apex of the Church. This dissipation of the consistory was the prelude to its complete emasculation, with a complementary excessive emphasis on the personal nature of papal authority, eliminating any mechanism for co-ordination and synthesis from the central government of the Church, abolishing the distinction between *causae maiores* and bureaucratic affairs which for centuries had formed the basis for the division of responsibility and competence between the legislature on one side and the executive arm on the other. Finally, the reform provided the occasion for a number of 'political' changes which an effective consistory would have made far less easy to push through.[4]

3. THE 'SISTINE' CURIA

So what, basically, did the Roman curia look like on the threshold of the modern era? It was a complex of offices, functions and tribunals born and developed in different curcumstances and following differing models, often with increased or superimposed responsibilities. These responsibilities did not yet actually extend to all aspects of the life of the Church, and certainly not to pastoral needs, but were rather the product of particular circumstances, such as the Congregation for the Council, which was typically post-Tridentine, or the inquisition, expressedly anti-Protestant, or the Secretariat of State itself, entrusted with political relationships with outside States. There was another group of congregations responsible for the affairs of the Church States, of which the pope was temporal sovereign. So the original nuclei of administrative and financial offices had been augmented by others, designed to help the pope with the new matters he had to deal with. Despite the fact that these new matters were qualitatively different, in that they were much more closely concerned with the spiritual life of the Chuch, the new congregations did not have an *ad hoc* structure to enable them to cope with them, but were all based on the same administrative-bureaucratic model; this applied as much to the Inquisiton as to the office responsible for provisions for the Papal States and to Propaganda Fide, set up in 1622 to administer mission territories.

Relations between these congregations and the pope, after the Sistine reform, were principally through a personal audience with the head of each congregation. This exacerbated the distinction between the legislative process and the executive phase, a distinction previously formalised by the deliberations of the consistory. What happened was that relations between the pope and the curia acquired a double strand of interweaving: the curia showed an increasing tendency to identify itself with the pope, and it also became increasingly possible for the curia to influence the decisions of the pope 'from within', and therefore invisibly— irresponsibly in the strict sense of the word. The Sistine concept of the central government of the Church postulated that it was the responsibility of the pope in person to have an overall view of the global problems of the Church and therefore to co-ordinate the actions of the curia. Experience has shown this to be more of a juridico-ecclesiastical presumption than a real possibility. In practice the central government of the Church was gradually taken over by the various congregations and in particular by the Secretariat of State and the (Supreme) Congregation of the Holy Office.

This structure, of which the nuncios provide an important peripheral ramification, has marked the western Church of the Roman communion with a strongly bureaucratic stamp in the modern age; highly developed and highly conscious of its own importance, it has above all given the Church a strongly universalist outlook. So in the long periods when Catholicism has been forced on to the defensive, withdrawing into itself like a beseiged citadel, the Roman curia, with a conviction bordering on arrogance, has reaffirmed its own right to guide the Church on a universal level. So the impossibility of achieving an effective universality has tended to accentuate the development of internal uniformity within Catholicism, maintaining that the unification of the Church on the basis of one historical model is a sure basis for future expansion. As is clear, this view has become more and more inadequate, not to say theologically indefensible and historically untenable. What it has done is cause a notable expansion of the area occupied by the curia and its congregations: any argument that can produce discussion on uniformity has become a *causa maior,* in which the curia has the right, not to say the duty, to intervene. It is not difficult to see how this has led to the progressive diminution of the freedom and responsibility of the bishops and their churches, and also—paradoxically—of the pope, whenever he has tried to introduce any significant innovation in the life of the Church. In-detectibly, the different offices have acquired a position and prestige disproportionate to their importance; they have become strongholds of tradition, conceived as the endless repetition of the same series of actions, in a typical process of bureaucratic deformation. One cannot but recognise that this undue expansion has made possible—and to a certain extent caused—the corresponding atrophy of the true centres of decision-making.

4. THE REFORM OF PIUS X

With the nineteenth century there came a renewed call for the reform of the Roman curia, based on the need better to distinguish between spiritual responsibilities and temporal ones relating to the Church as a State. This call, made more insistent by the loss of the Papal States, developed into a demand for the congregations to slacken the bonds of their powers and face up to new problems posed by the secularisation of contemporary society, as exemplified in marriage, for example. This led in 1908 to the reform decreed by Pius X, which cut out the 'temporal' congregations, set up a Congregation of the Sacraments to combat the secularisation of marriage, and tried to rationalise the responsibilities of each congregation. On a broader historical front, the reform of Pius X coincided with the far-reaching decision to combat legal disorders by drawing up *ex novo* a Codex for the whole Church, with Rome's hard-fought battle against Modernist tendencies, soon extended to a refutation of any sort of dynamic relationship between history on one hand and Christian revelation and the Church on the other. It is interesting to observe how at this time, in the absence of any co-ordinating and decision-making body, the leadership not only of the curia but of the whole government of the Church was taken over by the Consistorial Congregation, by virtue of the dynamic personality of Cardinal Da Lai and the trust reposed in him by Pius X. The titles of the principal proceedings of this congregation between 1908 and 1911 alone demonstrate the casual nature of this leadership, not to say the completely indeterminate character of the responsibilities exercised by the congregation itself.[5] The reform of Pius X therefore seems to have achieved very little. What it showed to be still alive and well was the 'jungle' nature of the curial structure, stubbornly resistant to any discipline, to which it was able to oppose the radical resistance of its random hierarchical structure. It lacked any internal coherence based on objectives and accepted distinctions, but it also lacked any clear delineation of its responsibilities toward the pope on one hand and the Church on the other. The identification of the curia with papal prerogatives and the acceptance of the personal supra-ecclesial status of the pope between created a vicious spiral.

The Codex of 1917

The Codex of Canon Law, promulgated in 1917 without a corresponding meeting of the bishops to approve it, sanctioned this state of affairs, can. 7 declaring that: 'By Apostolic Holy See, the Codex refers not only to the Roman Pontiff, but also, except where the subject matter or argument indicate otherwise, the congregations, tribunals and offices through which the Roman Pontiff himself meets the needs of the universal Church'. Next, under Ch. VII of Part I, entitled 'Supreme power and who participates in it under ecclesiastical law', heading IV—after that devoted to the pope, the ecumenical council and the cardinals—dealt with the Roman curia (chs. 242-62). Then followed canons on papal legates, patriarchs and metropolitans, local councils, etc. In this way the responsibilities of the curia came to be seen as co-existent with those of the pope, including (can. 220) 'all affairs of major importance, called *causae maiores* either from their own nature or from dispositions of the laws'. Within these unlimited responsibilities only particularly grave or extraordinary matters were previously reserved to the pope (can. 244, § 1); all ordinary or less grave matters could automatically be handled by the curia. The same distinction also applied to rulings, which required papal approval only if they related to matters outside the special faculties of the officials of the congregations (can. 244, § 2). The only conclusion one can draw is that all the ordinary business of the government of the Church was entrusted to the curia, with no control even on the part of the pope, except perhaps when he came to nominate curial officials, but even here his freedom was circumscribed by the expectations based on the 'careers' of high curial dignitaries. Canons 247 to 257 each dealt with one of the congregations, 258 and 259 with the tribunals, and 260 to 264 with the offices. The interlocking responsibilities of the highest officers was to guarantee information and co-ordination.[6]

If one tried to build an image of the Church on the basis of the spheres of responsibility of the congregations, it would indeed be a strange and disturbing image. Next to doctrine (Holy Office) came higher ecclesiastical offices (Consistory), sacramentary discipline (!?) and in particular that of marriage (Sacraments), discipline of the lower secular clergy and the people (Council), friars, monks and secular institutes (Religious). But all these aspects in the context of missionary countries came under a different authority (*Propaganda Fide*) and yet another in the Uniate Eastern Churches (*Orientale*). Then came rites, ceremonies and canonisations (Rites), papal ceremonial (Ceremonial), relations with outside governments (Extraordinary Ecclesiastical Affairs), and studies in seminaries and Catholic Universities (Seminaries and Universities). The Secretariat of State was an organ available for personal interventions by the pope, particularly in political matters.[7]

Anyone using this structure as a sole source of information would have some difficulty in finding a basis for an image of the Church, let alone a pastoral image of the Church, as a communion of ecclesiastical communities. The concept of the Church as a people nowhere emerges from this scarcely coherent and obviously defective mosaic of responsibilities. The congregations knew only partial and sectional aspects of the real Church, which they were liable to confuse with the Church as a whole, of which neither the individual congregations nor the curia as a whole had any realistic, overall appreciation. This must be one of the main reasons for the curia's atavistic fear of councils, feared as an alternative power centre, but above all seen as a 'monstrous' image of the Church, really because they could only be seen as a totality. On the other hand, the 'periphery' of the Church regarded the curia as alien because it could not see how it fitted in to the real structure of the Church.

5. THE REFORM OF THE CURIA IN VATICAN II

Once Pope John had announced a new Council, the preparatory documents collected from the bishops contained numerous and lively comments on the Roman curia. Above all, its excessive power was deplored, as was the arrogance of its dealings with the bishops, and the Italian monopoly; reforms were called for to promote its decentralisation, internationalisation and clarification of its responsibilities and procedures, so that the curia could become imbued with the spirit of service to the churches and the advancement of pastoral needs. During the last years of the pontificate of Pius XII, alarming symptoms of a hidden but violent rift between the pope and the curia were becoming apparent; John XXIII found dealings with the curia equally difficult. More than a battle for rights and responsibilities, this was rather a confrontation between two conceptions of the Church: that of the pope, an organic view guided by pastoral ideals, and that of the curia, political and empirical in tone; one dynamic, the other static; the first inspired by fidelity to the gospel, the second dominated by a pessimistic traditionalism. The confrontation came to a head when the curia jealously claimed a monopoly of preparatory work for the council and engaged in a titanic struggle to promulgate its own view of the Church. Unexpectedly, Pope John backed away from a hand-to-hand struggle and fought at a distance, saying merely that the bishops meeting in council would enjoy all the freedom to which they were entitled. The outcome, when all the preparatory *schemae* except that on the liturgy were thrown out, was a historic defeat for the curia. It had claimed the ability to map out an overall renewal of the Church and had failed, proving itself incapable of interpreting the mind of the Church and of guiding its life.[8]

Against this background, Vatican II prepared to tackle the task of reforming the curia at the beginning of the Second Session, on the occasion of the debate on the *schema* concerning bishops and the administration of dioceses. A preparatory sub-commission had sent a document *'De pastorali episcoporum munere deque cura animarum'* to press in 1962. Paragraph iv of Chapter I in this document dealt with the bishop as collaborator with the pope in the government of the universal Church, but the mode and objectives of this collaboration were totally deceptive. It spoke of collaboration in support of the persecuted churches, or of the missions, or of particular dioceses, but ended by giving pride of place to a 'Pastoral Centre' already existing attached to the Congregation of the Council. Everything was limited to individual contact between each bishop and the pope, and anything relevant to the normal business of running the Church was excluded even from this.

Then came the opening of the Council, the first session and the directives given by Pope John at the end of this for a substantial revision of the work of the preparatory commissions. Following this, at the end of April 1963, the Secretary of State, as president of the co-ordinating commission, sent two *schemae* for decrees to the Council, one on bishops and one on the care of souls, which later became fused into the Decree on the Bishops' Pastoral Office in the Church (*Christus Dominus*). Both tried to lay down norms relative to the relationship between the bishops and the government of the universal Church. The *schema* on bishops devoted its first chapter to the relationship between the bishops and the sacred congregations of the Roman curia, and para. 11 of the document on the care of souls was supposed to deal with the bishop as collaborator with the pope. So not the slightest step had been taken toward a more realistic approach to problems involved in this delicate aspect of the structure of the Church. It may seem incredible, but even now, in the interval between the first and second sessions of the Council, it was still maintained that the height of the bishops' participation in the central government of the Church could be attained by sending some of their members to participate in the Roman congregations and in the co-ordinatory function of the Pastoral Centre of the Congregation of the Council.

This paradoxical situation was only resolved thanks in the first place to the firm stand taken by the majority in the debate on the *schema* on the constitution of the Church. With the realisation that more than eighty per cent of the fathers agreed to the principle that 'The order of bishops is the successor to the college of the Apostles in teaching authority and pastoral rule. . . . Together with its head, the Roman Pontiff, and never without this head, the episcopal order is the subject of supreme and full power over the universal Church' (LG 22c), the ecclesiology of Vatican II took a basic and decisive step forward, which was to have repercussions on various aspects of the teaching of the Council, laying the foundations for a healthy process of reform.

The clarificatory effects of the understanding reached on the doctrinal level were soon felt in the debates in the hall, which on November 5th 1963 turned to the *schema* on bishops and diocesan administration. The initial general discussion on the document already made it clear that it was absolutely essential for it to be subjected to basic revision, in order to bring it into line with the general ecclesiological orientation adopted by the Council. Cardinal Liénart recalled the hint dropped by Paul VI that some of the bishops might be associated with the pope in studying and carrying out the central administration of the Church, and proposed that the *schema* should include a chapter on the relationship between the episcopate and the pope.

The debate on this subject reached its peak between November 6th and 8th, when a whole series of interventions brought the entire problem of the form of the existing central government of the Church to light in a dramatic way. Particularly significant in this respect were the speeches of the Melchite Patriarch Maximos IV, Cardinal Lercaro, Cardinal

Rugambwa and the Archbishop of Florence.

The Melchite Patriarch drew attention to the need to reform the college of cardinals so as to change it into a college made up of a certain number of bishops from all over the world, representing the whole order of bishops, which could collaborate with the pope in the government of the Church. A college made up in this way would not only have to study and map out solutions to the great problems in the life of the Church, but also give rise to a smaller body, which would act as permanent adviser to the pope on matters relating to the daily administration of the Church.

In direct opposition to this proposal, the Archbishop of Florence proposed the following day that a new congregation be instituted within the Roman curia (superior to the Supreme Congregation of the Holy Office), which would function as co-ordinator and director of all the others. Finally, on November 8th, two cardinals, one from a European see with a very long tradition and the other from Africa, a continent on the threshold of a new Christian era, agreed that this whole complex matter should be studied in depth by a special commission working as closely as possible with the pope. In particular, the Cardinal Archbishop of Bologna insisted on pointing out that not all problems of the central administration of the Church concerned the college of bishops. There is also a 'personal' form of this administration and, besides the decision-making and legislative level, there is an administrative and executive level, on which problems of reform and adaptation to new requirements have arisen. In effect, he was saying that decisions can be taken either through a personal exercise of supreme power on the part of the pope, as became normal in the latter part of the last century, or through a collegiate exercise of power, as happened, for example, from eleventh to sixteenth centuries through the relationshop between the pope and the college of cardinals and the consistory. On the executive level, the problem is one of rationalising instruments that are often inadequate or defective, incapable of dealing with the increasingly complex questions with which they are faced, or which err through excess, as in the case of the congregations overstepping the limits of the areas of decision reserved to them.

It was pointed out with some force that problems of this magnitude would hardly be resolved, and no appreciable rationalisation, let alone reform, would be achieved, merely by inserting an American, African or Asian bishop in the different departments and other bodies.

On his own account, the African cardinal stated powerfully that the problems of the central government of the Church neither could nor should be posed as claims on the part of the bishops, as something due to them by way of satisfaction. The central problem was much more complex, and could only be resolved by considering the service all the various bodies are called upon to render, aiming at and depending on conformity between the Church and its Head, the only authentic *form,* toward which any *re-form* must tend.

In fact, the proposal for an *ad hoc* commission to work out the views of the Council on reform of the Roman curia was not favourably received either in the *aula* or by Paul VI. The pope, only a few weeks after his election, had devoted his long discourse of September 21st, to the curia and its reform, in which he stated the need for 'simplification and decentralisation, but at the same time amplification so as to carry out new duties'; in each case it was to be up to the curia itself to formulate and carry out the reforms needed.[9] In this way, the whole matter remained as expressed in paragraphs 8-10 of the Decree on the Pastoral Office of Bishops. In general, this had been a very significant and innovatory session, in that for the first time the Roman curia had been dealt with in the context of the responsibilities of bishops in their relationship to the universal Church, which was precisely the title of the first chapter of the Decree. This element, however, was inadequately developed and even virtually contradicted by the drafting of the paragraphs dealing with it; in particular, para. 9 states that the curia is the instrument of the pope, and therefore acts in his name and with his authority, though this is to be to the benefit of the Church and in the service of the bishops. There follows a wish on the part of the Council fathers that the departments of the curia be 'reorganised and better adapted to the needs of the times . . .', also that, 'in view of the pastoral role proper to bishops, the office of legates of the Roman Pontiff be more precisely determined'. The next paragraph contains three wishes detailing how this reorganisation might be carried out: through internationalisation of the membership of the departments, by the inclusion of diocesan bishops, and finally, by giving a greater hearing to lay people.[10]

It could be said that the mountain had brought forth a mouse, but one needs to remember the mood of those crucial weeks in autumn 1963, which marked a decisive change in the orientation of Paul's pontificate. To take two examples: para. 9 makes no mention of the distinction between normative, administrative and executive functions of which he had spoken in the discourse already quoted, and para. 10b has lost two significant points in the course of its elaboration—that the members of the curial congregations should be nominated by episcopal conferences and convoked to Rome for set periods of time. This new current of timidity flowed into the pope's discourse on November 18th 1965, in which the curia was said to be in need only of 'perfectioning', while there were 'no great needs for structural change', and in any case, any change should be 'slow and partial, as it needs to be'.[11]

6. THE 'PAULINE' REFORM

In effect, the Council was deprived of any right to intervene in the reform of the curia, which the pope reserved to himself as '*res sua*'. There followed a long series of pronouncements, starting with *Pastorale munus* of September 15th 1963, instituting the Synod of Bishops, and ending with *Quo aptius* of February 27 1973, which transferred the functions of the Apostolic Chancellery to the Secretariat of State. The most significant acts were the general reform of the curia (August 15 1967) and the relevant procedures (February 22 1968). So fifty years after the reform of Pius X and nearly four hundred years after the Sistine reform, the Pauline reform introduced a myriad structural modifications (titles, adjustments of responsibilities, mergers and separations, etc.), all, in the absence of any structural reform, revolving around a few points particularly dear to Paul VI himself.[12] These are: the five-year term of office for directorial functions, the inclusion of bishops as members of the congregations, international recruiting of officers, and finally, the creation of a *novissima* curia, that is, in relation to the 'traditional', i.e., medieval one, and the 'new' one added by Sixtus V. The five-yearly resignation of directors is an innovation brought about by the pope himself, since it does not seem to have been proposed by anyone else; this was to ensure periodical occasions for renewal, besides breaking the 'career' pattern. The inclusion of bishops as members of the 'plenary' bodies of the congregations has been substantially modified by the fact that these bishops were chosen by Rome, and by the fact that 'plenary' sessions are held only once a year and are allowed only to discuss the broad lines of policy for each congregation.[13] 'Internationalisation' has been tenaciously pursued, but events have proved it an inadequate means of de-bureaucratising the curia, while it does seem to have led to an impressive increase in the number of curial officials. . . . The point that could have had the most innovatory impact—in the wake of the creation of the Secretariat for Christian Unity by John XXIII—is the group of Secretariats and Commissions designated by the title 'most new'. These are three Secretariats (Laity, Non-Christians, Non-believers) and various Councils and Commissions (Laity, Justice and Peace, Theology, etc.) explicitly and formally responsible for pastoral spheres and problems rather than for administrative or juridical matters. For a start, these bodies had the chance to organise themselves on modern lines, discarding the anachronisms and distortions afflicting the congregations. The fact that some of these bodies had a diocesan bishop—who remained such—at their head, also promised the possibility of really achieving a different style of working.

After ten years, the overall characteristics of the Pauline reform can be assessed. The abandonment of a re-structuring, let alone of a re-thinking of the curia in terms of collegiate government of the Church, has taken the impetus and vigour away from the whole exercise, leading to results on a smaller scale than those envisaged by Paul VI himself. On the other hand, problems he did not wish to bring about have assumed ever greater importance, such as the ever-expanding size of the work force[14] and a new centralisation of authority in areas that a few years ago were immune from curial interference, such as lay organisations. The conciliar insistence that curial powers should be exercised 'in the service of' the bishops has not prevented the summary deposition of some bishops in a way that suggests the anti-modernist purge of the early part of the century. What has been confirmed once more is the impossibility of any reform coming from within the curia that would make it an instrument of service to the communion of Churches in a manner befitting the values of the gospel. The possibility of it serving a normally collegiate form of Church government seems to be even more remote. This is not a matter of personal or group resistance or unsuitability among its members, but a structural inadaptation going back to its origins. The curia in fact came into being as a personal adjunct to the bishop of Rome, performing an essentially centralising function, with secular aims only accidentally connected with pastoral concerns. It is becoming increasingly clear that its whole concept belongs to a phase in the life of the papacy and of the Church that is in the process of being abandoned and replaced.

7. CONDITIONS FOR A PASTORAL STRUCTURE IN CENTRAL SERVICES

So as not to fall into an ingenuous utopianism, this consideration of the necessary conditions will be developed in recognition of the fact that all the churches, and particularly the Catholic Church, will be unable to achieve inter-ecclesial communion without having recourse to common services. So it is not a matter of dreaming of a universal Church without a curia, but of recognising not only the possibility of but also the need for the ecclesial *koinónia,* with the episcopal college grouped round the bishop of Rome at its centre, to have the use of effective services proper to an ecclesiology of communion, guided by the principle of the divine shepherdship and therefore of the brotherhood of the churches. There are some conceptual and structural obstacles to overcome on this road if we are to avoid coming back to where we started from, i.e., a project for reforming the curia that is simply an attempt to put new wine in old bottles, and then is shocked when the wine promptly turns sour.

(a) The Option for an Ecclesiology of Communion

The first crucial obstacle to surmount concerns the alternative between a concept of the universal Church as a communion of individuals and a concept of the universal Church as a communion of local churches, each authentically a church on the gospel model. This is the image of the

Church proposed by Vatican II and many examples could be quoted in support of this thesis. For a start, there is the affirmation in LG 23 that the Mystical Body is '. . . the body of the churches': this takes on its full significance when seen in relation and in synergy with other affirmations, such as those that recognise the Church of Christ as present in 'legitimate local congregations . . . themselves called churches in the New Testament', which therefore place the basic being and principal manifestation of the local Church in the eucharistic assembly brought together under the presidency of the bishop, who governs it as 'vicar of Christ' (LG 26 and 27). There is the analogous statement in LG 13 that particular local churches hold their rightful places, retaining their own traditions, with graces and gifts that can be shared by all the People of God . . . and that this applies also to 'the infant churches (once they are) fully established'. All this takes on greater significance seen in relation to the further assertion that 'various churches . . . have in the course of time coalesced into several groups, organically united, which preserving the unity of faith . . . enjoy their own discipline, their own liturgical usage, and their own theological and spiritual heritage' (LG 23). Typical—though not the only—examples of these are the ancient patriarchal churches, 'parent-stocks of the faith'. So it would seem that the functions once assumed by the patriarchal churches—if not to exactly the same degree, then at least proportionately—could in the present and the future be taken on by new groupings of local churches, including that of forming a theological patrimony proper to each major cultural and religious area. The fact that the fruitfulness of this principle has been applied—in the Decree *Ad Gentes*—to areas like Africa and Asia not yet covered or 'taken up' by a particular incarnation of the Gospel should not prevent it from being applied equally to the various parts of old Christian Europe. Between Castile and the Low Countries, Sicily and Piedmont, Brittany and Westphalia, there are differences in religious history and spiritual temperament at least as great as those between Italy and Greece or Ireland. These differences cannot be ironed out by the single discipline of the Latin Church, with only minor and marginal divergencies, but should be able to express themselves with a controlled but creative dynamism capable of recomposing different areas not only on the basis of national divisions but according to the main threads of their spiritual history and their present cultural and religious experience, forming organically homogeneous groupings. Without an ecclesiological deepening of awareness of this tendency and a corresponding operational impetus, the horizon that gave birth to the curia will never be changed.

(b) The Implementation of Universal Jurisdiction

A second crucial point concerns the transmission to each bishop through the sacramental act of consecration as bishop of effective and inalienable participation in the governing of the universal Church. This has been called 'universal jurisdiction', but the theological fact is more important than the name. It means in fact recognising that each individual bishop has received directly from Christ a share in the *sollicitudo omnium ecclesiarum,* which care is designed to be exercised as part of the whole episcopal college presided over by the pope. This dimension cannot be subtracted from the episcopal office, any more than the responsibility of each bishop for the local community entrusted to him can be substantially diminished. This fact leads directly to a third basic consideration, relating to the principle of subsidiarity.

(c) Ecclesial Subsidiarity

This was much spoken of in the Council, and the expression is still very much in fashion, as if naming the principle alone was proof of an open mind and an ability to provide a correct interpretation of the relationship between the universal Church and the local churches, or at least of that between the Holy See and the episcopate.[15]

There is no denying that this can serve as an initial orientation; but it is a purely and generically sociological orientation equally applicable to any large and complex structure, and therefore only a general and imprecise approach to what is most particular in the constitutive structure and rule of the Church. In this structure and rule, the key principle is quite different, and far more *radically* based in the literal sense, far more demanding, and, in a way, far more permanent: it is the principle of the divine reality and functionality of the local community—particularly the community in the eucharistic act—in relation to the universal Church; the principle of the originality of particular charisms and spiritual experiences stemming directly from one and the same Holy Spirit, without the mediation of the universal Church community.

On the basis of this difference in structure, while in any other society the principle of subsidiarity can always be balanced for reasons of simple expediency by the *principium solidaritatis,* in the Church the balance between the proper vocation of the local church and the requirements of the universal Church cannot be determined by sociological evaluation, but requires a discernment of the Spirit; it is not merely a prudential fact, of the order of 'political' experience, but is mainly a charismatic fact, of the order of faith and the evangelical purity of those responsible for seeing it carried out.

So too much insistence on the principle of subsidiarity without an adequate reformulation of it, instead of clarifying the question in terms proper to it, risks reducing it to a lower plane and confusing it; instead of maturing ecclesiology, it diverts it into sociology.

(d) Abandonment of 'Causae maiores'

A theologically strict acceptance of the principle of subsidiarity would, amongst other things, require the abandonment of the concept of *causae maiores*. This is an expression of a universalist conception of the Church and the product of a history of centralisation; it must also be seen as incapable of serving differing needs. From the viewpoint of service to the communion of churches, a distinction between important matters (requiring central decisions) and non-important (which can be left to individual bishops) is inadequate, since we must recognise that every aspect of Christian and ecclesial life becomes the responsibility of each local Church and its ministers, even if we accept that some aspects or concerns of the life of the Church can be referred back, either as a matter of course or in exceptional circumstances, to be dealt with on the level of the regional or universal communion of churches.

As a first step, a clarification of the relations between the local churches and the Holy See would require a measure of identification and an approximate classification of legitimate special traditions which yet belonged within the overall one *catholic* tradition; not merely a simple distinction between eastern and western traditions, but also—even if by a lower analogy—the different traditions existing or in the process of growing up within the bosom of the western Church. This is the first condition—being theological and spiritual—for a pluralism of churches that will be more than purely nominal. If the new forms of contact and co-ordination are reduced to political instruments and individual diplomatic contacts, this will not guarantee the *proprium* of each local church and will merely serve to accentuate the abstract authority, though not the real efficacy, of the primacy of Rome.[16] It must be said that till now we have scarcely begun to make any sort of distinction between some of the major questions of faith (such as the reformulation of some of the great Christological doctrines) and purely disciplinary matters, whether of major importance (such as the celibacy of the clergy), of less importance but still of general concern, or, worse still, examination of individual cases.

It is therefore time to make a first attempt at a classification of a hierarchy of values, even if this takes time to establish. The criterion could be that used in the Decree on Ecumenism, that there is 'an order or "hierarchy" of truths, since they vary in their relationship to the foundation of the Christian faith' (UR 11). For convenience, and purely by way of example, these might be graded on the following scale:

(1) matters directly and formally pertinent to the central nucleus of the Christian faith (articles of the Symbol);

(2) matters directly and formally pertinent to the explicit and primary norms of revealed laws;

(3) matters pertaining to questions of faith and morals deriving from revelation, but less directly and formally included in the formal deposit of revelation and therefore conceding greater possibilities of being interpreted in different traditions;

(4) institutions and structures held to be of prime importance, but not of divine institution, (e.g., the celibacy of the priesthood);

(5) matters of prime importance concerning pastoral care and the liturgy;

(6) disciplinary matters of general application;

(7) major problems of relations with the civil power, to do with the social and cultural development of the contemporary world, on which a greater freedom of opinion is permissible;

(8) questions relating to matters covered by nos. 5, 6 and 7 in this classification, but of lesser importance;

(9) more particular matters, individual cases, etc.

The need to maintain contact and unity decreases rapidly as one goes down this scale, till it is finally obliterated by the greater need for a highly articulate pluralism; however, the solutions adopted in certain cultural and ecclesial areas, different in both space and time even when problems of capital importance are concerned, should not be ruled out *a priori*.

(e) The normative or legislative process

These observations would not be complete without one last point: any articulations differentiated by level of subject matter and ecclesiastical area will, at all levels, cut across a formal distinction which is at the same time one of substance—that between the forms of relationship between centre and periphery in matters relating to the executive and administrative process and those relating to the normative process.

If it is possible to see contact and eventual participation by the bishops in the executive and administrative process being brought about in a relationship with the curial offices, then the question has to be put: should the same form of contact and participation be applied indiscriminately to the normative process? Or should some other form not rather be worked out for this, something that would guarantee a continual *rapport* between the episcopate and the pope, over and above the curia? This would bring important practical consequences, the first of which would be the replacement of the synod of bishops by a deliberative body capable of acting as a genuine expression of episcopal collegiality.

This, it must clearly be stated, does not imply any lowering of the status of the primacy, or a restriction of the sphere in which it can operate.

Rather, it means raising the authority of the pope to the effective level of the major concerns of the universal Church, and the better realisation of his efficacy, enhanced by the direct and effective participation of the episcopate in its more proper function of universal legislator.

This direction is suggested by the present situation of the Church: what is being questioned is not so much the institution of the Church, where a strengthening of administrative bonds would be enough to answer certain manifestations of indiscipline and intolerance. What is under siege from all quarters today, both inside and outside the Church, is faith itself. In this situation it is more than ever necessary—as history and the experience of the Church have shown—to revindicate the need for the primacy and for the function most proper to Peter, to confirm his brethren in their faith (Luke 22:23). But it must be a primacy freed from the trappings of the pontifical monarchy, operating as the supreme charism in the guidance of the Church, for which the pope needs to be unencumbered with all inessential trappings (political, or merely relating to ecclesiastical administration and organisation), and restored to the fulness of his authority, above all as president in charity of the communion in faith and hope of the sister churches in their struggle with the world and the devil.

A rethinking of the possibility of services common to the churches in pastoral terms encounters an objective obstacle in the Roman curia. For many centuries this has been the body through which the pope exercised his personal control over a Church conceived on universalist lines. It does not seem capable of adequate adaptation to the new needs, by reason of the circumstances and principles surrounding both its origin and its development. It is now not a question of eliminating abuses or distortions, as was the case in the sixteenth century, but of setting out on a completely new course, one in keeping with the requirements of an ecclesiology of communion.

Translated by Paul Burns

Notes

1. One of the most authoritarian and triumphalistic expressions of this point of view is the address made by Cardinal Alfredo Ottaviani as Secretary of the Holy Office, in January 1961, on the occasion of the visit of Pope John XXIII to the congregation. Ottaviani, in fact, said: 'As rector of the first and foremost department of the Roman curia I consider myself entitled to express the joy, encouragement and gratitude which the visit of their head gives to the members of this singular and glorious body, the Roman curia: a body so glorious and ancient as to seem, in its initial impetus, contemporary with the Apostles; yet so new in its fervent, diligent and fruitful work that it seems to have been born yesterday' (*Osservatore Romano,* Jan 16-17 1961, p. 3). Though expressed more soberly, the historical premiss of the *Motu Proprio 'Regimini universalis ecclesiae'* betrays a similar attitude.

2. See throughout, G. Le Bras *Le Istituzioni Ecclesiastiche Della Cristianità Medievale* (Turin² 1974) pp. 465 ff; L. Pasztor 'L'histoire de la Curie romaine, problème d'histoire de l'Englise' in RHE 64 (1969) pp. 353-66; K. Weinzierl 'Die geschichtliche Entwicklung der Römischen Kurie' in *Ius Sacrum* (K. Mörsdorf zum 60 Geburtstag, Munich, 1969) pp. 275-93.

3. The most significant and systematic opposition to the reform of Sixtus V came from Card. Gabriele Paleotti, and was set out fully in his *De Sacri Consistorii Consultationibus,* published in 1592; cf P. Prodi *Il Cardinale Gabriele Paleotti* (Rome² 1967) pp. 441-3, 469-78, 479-526.

4. A significant case is that of the deliberations of the Congregation for the Greeks, which reduced the Christian community of the Greek tradition in Italy to a mere 'rite', instead of respecting its reality as a 'church'. The whole affair has been illuminatingly studied by V. Peri *Chiesa Romana e 'Rito' Greco. G. A. Santoro e la Congregazione dei Greci, 1566-1596* (Testi e richerche di scienze religiose, 9, Brescia 1975): 'The whole operation, while depending for its outcome on the detailed preparatory deposition made by Santoro to the Congregation for the Greeks, and while being possibly defensible on the basis of the pastoral urgency of certain actual situations, nevertheless remains something that, by reason of its objective historical components, goes beyond questions, however serious, of the ordinary internal administration of the Western Church. A curial Congregation, which, however authoritative and expert, is still a bureaucratic body, was not competent to find an adequate solution to a problem which . . . involved another church' (p. 205).

5. 'An idea of the mentality of the Consistorial Congregation directed by Cardinal De Lai can be gained from an analysis of the main decrees it issued between 1908 and 1911. Reduction of the competence of the Congregation of Propaganda, returning all cases concerning rites to the Congregation of Rites and all cases of missionary discipline to that of Religious (November 12 1908). Recommendation to bishops to transmit all documents concerning government to their trusted procurators under seal of secrecy (November 15 1908). All metropolitans deprived of the right to pass judgment and obliged to remit the case to the Roman Congregation (January 18 1909). Definition of the sphere of competence of Roman ecclesiastical tribunals (June 11 1909). Superiors for-

bidden to allow seminary students to read newspapers except those containing scientific matters contained in their syllabus (October 20 1910). Priests forbidden to engage in any financial matters except the rural savings banks (November 18 1910). Rigorous instructions on the obligation to swear the anti-Modernist oath (October 3 1910, December 17 1910, March 1 and 21 1911). Reservation to the Sacred Roman Congregation of the sole right to interpret the texts of the Council of Trent (February 11 1911). Prohibition to use Duchesne's *History of the Church* in seminaries (September 1 1911).' From L. Bedeschi *La Curia Romana Durante la Crisi Modernista. Episodi e Metodi de Governo* (Parma 1968) p. 64, n. 69. The volumes of *Romana Curia a b. Pio X Sapienti Consilio Reformata* (Rome 1951) give a predominantly apologetic view of the reform of 1908.

6. The project for revision of Canon Law provides a can. 7 on the curia similar to that of 1917. A new formulation placed under title I (*De suprema ecclesiae universae auctoritate eiusque exercitio*), heading I (*De Romano pontifice deque collegio episcoporum*) can. 156 § 3 declares: 'Romano pontifici praesto sunt quoque quae ad Curiam Romanum pertinent personae et instituta, ad quae spectat varia obire munia atque explere mandata quibus praescriptae ad bonum Ecclesiarum ordinationes directe ad effectum adducantur.' So the curia is once more placed in an exlusive relationship with the pope; the expressions used will repay any amount of reading.

7. It is useful to look through the volumes devoted every year to the *Attività della S. Sede,* which enables one to keep an eye on the activities of the curia. N. del Re *La Curia Romana* (Rome[3] 1970) is full of information, as is G. Delgado *La Curia Romana. El Gobierno Central de la Iglesia* (Pamplona 1973). But for an organic treatment of the curia it is still necessary to go back to D. Bouix *Tractatus de Curia Romana* (Paris 1880).

8. See G. and A. Alberigo *Giovanni XXIII. Profezia Nella Fedeltà* (Brescia 1978).

9. AAS 55 (1963) 798-9.

10. On the whole of this matter, the volume on *La Charge Pastorale des Évêques* (Paris 1969) is, unfortunately, quite unsatisfactory.

11. AAS 57 (1965) 980-81.

12. See the analysis by J. Sánchez y Sánchez, 'La constitution apostolique *Regimini ecclesiae universae* six ans après' in *L'Année Canonique* 20 (1976) pp. 33-66, which maintains that this reform has not respected the criteria indicated by the Council. J. Gordon 'De curia romana renovata; renovatio; desiderata et renovatio facta conferuntur', in *Periodica de re Morali, Liturgica, Canonica* 58 (1969) pp. 59-116, is devoid of critical value.

13. The Regulation of the Curia, published February 22 1968, lays down that the bishop members of the various congregations do not form part of the Ordinary Congregation nor of the Congress, which are the regular decision-making bodies of the congregations themselves (AAS 60 [1968] arts. 111-2 and 123).

The subordinate position of the bishop is emphasised once more in the document on the process of canonisation (*Sanctitas clarior* of March 19 1969), according to which a bishop cannot institute a cause for canonisation without previous assent from the Holy See (ASS 61 [1969] I/3). The same spirit is shown in a 1972 Instruction (*Episcoporum delectum*) on the procedure to be followed in the nomination of bishops. Having recognised that it is appropriate for the episcopal conference to suggest candidates for nomination to the Holy See, it is laid down that the Nucio (art. XIII) should present the *terna* from which the final choice is made (AAS 64 [1972] 391).

14. According to S. Sanz Villalba, 'La curia romana, órgano de administración de la Iglesia' in *Rev. Esp. de Derecho Canónico* 17 (1972) p.772, in 1900 the curia had 185 officials, and in 1932, 205. By 1961 the number had risen to 1,322, by 1967 to 2,866, and to 3,146 by 1977. See G. Zizola 'Le pouvoir romain: centralisation et burocratisation dans l'église catholique' in *Lumière et Vie* 26 (1977) p. 27.

15. Since an article by W. Bertrams 'De principio subsidarietatis in iure canonico' in *Per. de re Morali, Lit., Can.,* 46 (1957) pp. 3-65, which ascribed the caution shown by Pius XII in applying this principle to the Church to his fear of weakening the hierarchical structure, it has become gradually more fashionable: O. Karrer 'The principle of subsidiarity in the Church' in G. Baraúna (ed.) *The Church of Vatican II* (London and New York 1966); M. Kaiser 'Das prinzip der Subsidiarität in der Verfassung der Kirche' in *Archiv für Katholisches Kirchenrecht* 133 (1964) pp. 3-13; there is also the address by Card. Felici to the Synod of Bishops of 1967 and then: F. Salerno 'Canonizazione del principio di subsidiarietà' in *La collegialità Episcopale per il Futuro Della Chiesa* (Florence 1969) pp. 138-48; and, finally, R. Metz 'La subsidiarité, principe régulateur des tensions dans l'église' in *Rev. de Droit Can.* 22 (1972) pp. 155-72.

16. In dealing with problems on this level it is important to realise that 'technical' proposals and suggestions concerning better exchange of information between the centre and local bodies will only lead to progress if they are carried out in the right spirit. That is, only if they are conceived and guided by an ecclesiological doctrine and consciousness in accord with the broad principles of the Council. Otherwise there is the danger that reciprocal information, which necessarily strengthens the centre, can be diverted through a diversity of objectives into becoming an instrument of greater centralisation, control and uniformity.

If technical innovations are not accompanied by a deep renewal of the ecclesiological conscience of the central bodies, the very material improvement in means of communication and the speeding-up of dialogue between the central offices in Rome and the peripheral practitioners can lead to a weightier conditioning of the originality, special gifts and specific traditions of the local churches.

Part II

The Reality of Centralising Institutions

Gregorio Delgado del Rio

The Organisation of the Church's Central Government

'IN THE supreme, full and immediate exercise of his power over the Church, the Roman Pontiff makes use of the departments of the Roman curia . . . for the good of the Church and the service of pastors' (*Christus Dominus,* 9). Thus it 'offers the Vicar of Christ the practical possibility of fulfilling the apostolic duty he owes to the whole Church' (John Paul I). However the curia's present structure does not seem to be fully in accord with the spirit of the Council and it is not adapted to the pastoral needs of the moment. To fulfil the Council's requirements far-reaching reform is urgent. But how is such a reform to be achieved?

1. PRIMARY CONSIDERATIONS

1. As we pointed out a few years ago, the figure of the pope, in the light of the Council's ideas, must be presented in terms of the primary and essential nature of the papal office. We need 'to identify with increasing precision what there is about this "ministry" that is particular and specific' (John Paul II). There is of course no doubt that the papal ministry bears a strict relation to the very nature of the Church, as 'principle and foundation' of the unity of faith and communion, and supreme guarantee of the 'single divine constitution of the Church' and of its saving mission in the world. This function as head of the Church in its pastoral rule, in the magisterium, and in the call to holiness cannot be abandoned or transferred. The pope must exercise it personally with the greatest possible dedication.

However there is a nucleus of functions, which were originally ascribed to the pope, which he does not necessarily have to fulfil personally. These functions can be delegated, and this delegation can be organised in any way which most efficiently fulfils these specifically papal functions. At this point we should remember that many habitual aspects of the papacy are merely historical forms. We must avoid the frequent mistake of identifying, without qualification, the function of the pope with the collection of functions historically fulfilled by the Roman curia. In any case the central government of the Church must be at the service of the specifically papal function.

2. The importance of the diocesan bishop as described by the Council has still not been given its due weight. The autonomy of local churches requires, in order to belong to the constitutional order, the effective exercise of decentralised legal jurisdiction. The diocesan bishop, 'the visible principle and foundation of unity in his particular church' (LG, 23) must be empowered really and truly to exercise all those functions and powers which 'are necessary to the fulfilment of his pastoral office' (CD, 8). In this context we should include Paul VI's statement that 'most pastoral problems can find an appropriate solution' within the local church. But in order to make this work, a radical organisational change is necessary, with direct repercussions on the content and meaning of the functions usually fulfilled by the Roman curia. Many of these functions more properly belong to the diocesan bishops. The Roman curia ought to fulfil functions which tend 'to guarantee the authenticity and unity of faith, the work of charity, the most perfect possible harmony between the living members of the undivided Church of Christ' (Paul VI). These functions are closely connected with the papal function, in whose apostolic service the Roman curia collaborates.

In principle, anything that can be organised, regulated or directed by the local churches should not be withdrawn from their competence and centralised in the Roman curia. The safeguarding of the necessary unity of faith and communion, guaranteed by the pope, does not require that the Roman curia should have powers which go beyond this basic goal and which in fact impose uniformities on the whole Church which are not necessarily justifiable. The function of the Roman curia should be very different from what it is at present, if the constitutional rights of the diocesan bishop are to be taken seriously. The Roman institutional bodies must ensure 'the articulated organisation of legitimate autonomies, contained within an indispensable respect for essential unity of discipline as also of faith' (John Paul I). But in order to do this they do not need all the powers they have at present.

3. Faithful to the spirit of the Council, the most recent popes have plainly expressed their clear will to give the college of bishops the power

to collaborate more effectively in the government of the universal Church. The problem is to develop adequate institutions to canalise effectively the growing force of the college of bishops. In this context, the synod of bishops is asked to turn itself into a key institution as an instrument capable of offering criteria and programmes for the working of government, which is very different work from attending to daily pastoral needs.

4. *'Utilitas ecclesiae vel fidelium'* or *'bonum dominici gregis'*, the supreme reason for all the Church's action, must determine how the Council's doctrine can gradually be put fully into practice.

This requires an assessment of the actual state of the Church in this historical moment. This assessment, in which the college of bishops can be of vital assistance to the pope, must be the key to determining the way in which the constitutional rights of bishops can most prudently and conveniently be developed, even if this means the elimination of ancient juridical and organic schemata (viz. taking powers away from the curia). The right choice must be made to suit current circumstances. Great clarity of vision is necessary so that an efficient structure may be built on sound foundations.

2. THE PROBLEM

Once these principles have been established, the problem then becomes technical. How best to organise the working of government at the level of the universal Church? What structure should be set up? What should be the system of relationships between the various organs of government? The answer to these questions cannot be given by theology, or pastoral theology. It is strictly technical.

I think this way of looking at the problem is of fundamental importance if mistakes are not to be made. Good organisation of the government of the universal Church will not come from expressions of good will or from a juridical system the definition of which makes frequent use of the term 'pastoral'. Government structures are not pastoral but juridical. They have a specific internal, strictly technical, dynamism. To think otherwise is unhelpful utopianism. If what is required is to *organise* the central government of the Church, then *particular organising techniques must be employed.*

3. SPECIAL POINTS

Any serious attempts to organise the central government of the Church must cope, among others, with the following questions:

1. It must differentiate between different functions (executive, con-

sultative, judicial) and fix their respective relationships. Within the function of executive government it must *name* each and every one of the organs of government to put an end to the present ambiguities. How many are there? The reply to this question will be in accordance with the choice of organisation that has been made previously, and the degree of efficiency it seeks.

2. It must determine as rigourously as possible the sphere and competence of each of these organs of government. This is the only way to avoid permanent sources of conflict and malfunctioning, and ensure the necessary co-ordination between the different government bodies.

3. A body needs to be set up whose specific function, among others, would be the effective co-ordination of these different government bodies. The lack of provisions for co-ordination in the present system is only too obvious. Only a supreme Council of Government, which we proposed some time ago, would be capable of resolving these difficulties.

4. The de-centralising process of the function of government must be done in such a way that it avoids the inconveniences which are bound to arise in the very nature of 'vicarhood'. I think it is vital to state very clearly that the organs of government, within their own sphere, are solely responsible for their own acts and all their consequences (control). It is very important to distinguish between the acts of the pope and those of the Roman curia. There are techniques by which this could be done without detriment to the papal function.

5. In accordance with the specific nature of the office of primate, in whose service the Roman curia collaborates, the organs of government must have both directing and restraining functions. They must initiate, encourage and help activities, and at the same time keep watch that these activities are in conformity with the unity of faith and communion, and with the nucleus of the Church, on the basis of Church discipline which has previously been set out in an unambiguous manner.

6. The internal order of the different organs of government must be such as to create the greatest efficiency in the exercise of their functions. Thus I think it is vital to break up the present internal structure of the Roman departments and seek a more flexible and functional order.

7. The Secretariat of State, as at present, should be regarded as a key body within the central government of the Church, but it should be institutionalised and regulated within the whole organisational complex.

8. The personnel serving in this system of government should be recruited in accordance with the qualifications necessary to fulfil posts at different levels. Every government body needs its own 'staff', qualified to fulfil its functions properly. This would then make it possible radically to rethink the problem of the numerous pontifical commissions.

9. Whatever system of government is adopted, and whatever cor-

responding structure is set up to put it into operation, I think it is necessary that it should be laid down legally, in the form of a constitution, which could be available for consultation at all levels. I do not think that this written constitution should be omitted from the process of reform of general canon law.

Translated by Dinah Livingstone

Giancarlo Zizola

Secretariats and Councils of the Roman Curia

SELDOM IN its history has the curia been so enlarged and strengthened as it was by Paul VI's reform, which had important lasting effects on the structure of papal government. This reinforcement of the curia happened at a time when sociologists foresaw the breaking down of bureaucracy, and religious institutions were becoming less important to religious people of the twentieth century.

In 1961 the 'curials' numbered 1,322. In 1978 there were 3,146 of them, an increase of 1,824, so that the size of Pope John's curia was more than doubled.

The greatest expansion was in the political and diplomatic sections, concentrated in the Secretariat of State. In the last ten years this has increased from 77 to 114 officials. The Secretariat of State is also the least internationalised body in the curia: 91 out of the present 114 officials are Italians. Two-thirds of the present staff have taken office since 1967. A new development has been the appointment of a large number of men in religious orders, at present 22. The reinforcement of the political structures at the top of the Church adds to its general politicisation: many officials, after working in the Secretariat of State, go abroad as papal nuncii. Then they return to Rome as heads of departments in the curia and are made cardinals, which means they have the right to elect the pope. This is a spiral which is the mainspring of papal politics.

As most analysts have observed, this means that the function of the cardinal secretary of state, which used to be seen as a mainly ecclesial and religious one through its links with the bishops, has lost its governing role.

The synod of bishops no longer has power to make decisions on the general government of the Church; this has passed to politicians. Moreover by this reform the Secretariat of State acquired great power of ruling and controlling because of its immediate contact with the pope, which seriously affected the balance of power both within the curia and in relation to the universal Church. As the reform intended, the 'separate bodies' were neutralised, but the result was more hierarchy leading up to strengthening of the personal, absolute and exclusive power of the pope as ruler of the universal Church. Surrounding bishops had obtained access to the direction of departments. But at the same time these departments were subordinated to the Secretariat of State. And alone among the curial bodies, the Secretariat of State excluded surrounding bishops. This internal monarchical structure has caused a duplication of the work of the departments: the Secretariat of State contains liturgical and legal sections, sections to deal with questions about the clergy, economic questions and the press. Every document prepared by one of the departments has to be submitted to it, to be scrutinised by further experts who are above the departments and secret from them, and there is no appeal except to the pope himself. We might well ask whether this reduplicated curia, the Secretariat of State, should not be a sufficient instrument of government of the pope in itself, like the Apostolic Secretariat which in 1487 represented the nucleus of the curial organisation. But at the top, surrounded by his personal bureaucracy, papal power becomes submerged in a mountain of paperwork: the reform bureaucratised the central governing body of the papacy, so that it was difficult for this body to be free for its more important task of pastoral oversight. The Council for Public Affairs of the Church is in charge of the papacy's foreign policy: under Paul VI their work was greatly increased but there was only a moderate increase in staff, 36 as opposed to 30 ten years ago. However Vatican foreign diplomacy has been expanded greatly, both in structure and personnel. This has contributed to the growth of the central apparatus of papal government, but it has not grown as fast as other sectors. There are 16 new bodies and commissions which have extended the papal sphere of interest and intervention. The officials of these 'new curias' which have sprung up beside the original curia, number 144, about a hundred more than in 1967, when there were only six new bodies. In addition, recruitment is rather more international than in the historical departments. These new bodies are much smaller than the old departments, which vary in size from 25 (the Congregation of Bishops) to 70 (the Evangelisation of Nations). Each of the new bodies has no more than a dozen officials.

Here we restrict ourselves to speaking briefly about the five larger bodies among these 'new curias', the three Secretariats (for Christian

Unity, for Non-Christians and for Non-believers), the Council for the Laity and the Pontifical Commission 'Justitia et Pax'. They were founded soon after the Vatican Council, in the hope of bringing about ecclesiastical reform by creating new structures. The idea was to set up a second curia to engage in 'dialogue' with the autocratic curia, to promote cultural interchange so that the eurocentric and defensive curial ideology might go through a process of crisis and transformation and reach wider, more universal horizons. The initiator of this plan was John XXIII who first set up the Secretariat for Christian Unity in 1960. The idea was suggested to him by L. Jaeger, the archbishop of Paderborn, and worked out and put into practice by Cardinal A. Bea, who was thus authorised to give official blessing to the ecumenical movement in Rome. In 1964 Paul VI set up the Secretariat for Non-Christians, and in 1965 the Secretariat for Non-believers, thus institutionalising the ideas in his first encyclical 'Ecclesiam suam'. The object of these Secretariats was to promote dialogue. The Council for the Laity was set up in 1967 and more firmly established in 1976, at the same time as the 'Justitia et Pax' Commission, also set up in 1967 and confirmed in 1976, in spite of strong opposition.

Here we cannot attempt to assess the effect these bodies have had on the official curia. But we can say that they have been hampered in their work by their subordinate position (except perhaps the Unity Secretariat) and that their attempt to penetrate the cultural fastness of the curia has largely been a failure. Only Cardinal Willebrands, the president of the Secretariat for Christian Unity, is a member of the Congregation for Doctrine, and only Cardinal Oopilio Rossi, the president of the Council for the Laity, is a member of the Council for the Church's Public Affairs and the Congregation of Bishops. The only historical Congregation of which the heads of the three Secretariats are members is the Congregation for Evangelisation. Otherwise they have been diverted to less important Congregations, while the dominant group of cardinals in the historical curia remains very inbred. The secretaries of the new bodies are not even consulted, as a rule, in the decision-making of the historical Congregations, except the Congregation for Evangelisation. Only the secretary for the Secretariat for Non-believers, V. Miano, is a consultant for the Holy Office. On the other hand, the secretaries for five Congregations (Eastern Church, Evangelisation, Bishops, Religious, Clergy) are consultants to the Council for the Laity. This impression of lack of communication is probably also due to the small production of documents by the new Institutes as a counter-weight to the documents produced by the historical Congregations and the papal magisterium. Quite often the Secretariat for Christian Unity has had to intervene, as an extreme measure, to demand modifications, at least in style, in documents produced by the Congregation for Doctrine which were not ecumenical in tone. The intervention of the Secretariat for Non-believers on Paul VI's 'Evangelii nuntiandi' and the Directorate of Bishops had very slight effect and the Secretariat's line was quite different on Vatican politics towards officially atheist states. The Council for the Laity expresses the rank reached by the laity in the Catholic Church—still a subordinate one to the hierarchy—but it has not succeeded in expressing the importance of the laity's position in the Church in relation to the central apparatus of government. The 'Justitia et Pax' Commission was forced to resolve a crisis at the cost of its total submission to the political dominance of the Secretariat of State, and its president, the African Cardinal Gantin, was removed from his diocese and cut off in Rome. There are different attitudes and ways of working in the central government and the present problem is to see whether any real communication between ancient and new institutions and interests can overcome the tendency to travel along parallel routes, with one set of institutions having power over the other without any interchange between them.

The new bodies are blackmailed by lack of funds—threatened with axing—because they are made to pay for the Vatican financial crisis and they bear the brunt of the cut in the expensive central bureaucratic apparatus. The Secretariat for Non-believer's funds in 1978 were 21 million lire (approximately $24,000 or £12,000) and an attempt was made to integrate this Institute with the Secretariat for Non-Christians to reduce personnel. This latter Institute—which also has a Commission for relations with Islam—has an annual budget of 14 million lire (approximately $18,000 or £9,000) and the Secretariat for Christian Unity—with its autonomous Commission for Relations with Judaism—is not much better off. However, there has in fact been an increase in personnel from 1967 to 1978: the Secretariat for Unity—presided over by Cardinal J. Willebrands, Archbishop of Utrecht—has increased from 11 to 19 officials (5 Italians and 14 non-Italians), the Secretariat for Non-Christians, presided over by Cardinal S. Pignodoli, has increased from 6 to 9 (5 Italians and 4 non-Italians), the Secretariat for Non-believers, presided over by Cardinal Koenig, has increased from 4 to 8 (3 Italians and 5 non-Italians). The Council for the Laity has 18 officials (10 Italians), an increase of 13. 'Justitia et Pax' has 15 (only 2 Italians and 13 non-Italians), whereas in 1967 it had only one. The new curia is badly funded, even though its functions are potentially more universally important then the old curia's because they go beyond the functioning and internal problems of the Church's administration. But although the new curia contains very gifted people both in theology and pastoral experience, there has been a tendency for the same people to stick in the same places during the last ten years. In general we have not seen many new faces.

And these old hands in the new Institutes are beginning to feel worn down by the sense of isolation, even though the work of cultural change in which they are engaged needs a long time to take effect.

Translated by Dinah Livingstone

Zenon Grocholewski

The Function of the Sacred Roman Rota and the Supreme Court of the Apostolic Signatura

1. THE SACRED ROMAN ROTA

THE CONSTITUTION *Regimini Ecclesiae Universae* did not change the powers of the Sacred Rota except accidentally. The principal job of the court continues to be the hearing—in the third and last instance, and to a lesser extent in the second instance—of cases referred by appeal to the Holy See. The great majority of these cases are applications for the declaration of the nullity of marriage.

In this work the Sacred Rota has a double important function:

1. Its primary function is to be a court of appeal staffed by experts, to which a Catholic who feels that his local court has not done him justice, has the right to appeal. Of course it would be absurd to call such a function offensive to the status of diocesan and inter-diocesan courts. No judgment is infallible and therefore it cannot claim that there is no reason for it to be reviewed. The existence of courts of appeal which can overturn the verdict of lower courts is allowed in all juridical systems and is one of the ways of safeguarding the rights of the defendant.

Of course if it is to fulfil this function efficiently it is necessary for the Sacred Rota to deal with cases without too great a delay. If a Catholic were put off appealing to this court for fear of an enormous delay, or if his matrimonial problem were to lie heavy on his conscience and was aggravated by a long wait for a decision by the Holy See, this would mean that the court was not working properly, and that reform was needed. With all due respect, it appears that cases referred to the Sacred Rota are often subject to long delays.[1]

2. A second important function for the Sacred Rota is to give legal help to other courts. Not all dioceses have the necessary experts available, and not all dioceses offer scope for the acquisition of the necessary experience. They often have too much other work to do and their court work is a tiny part of their activity. So a higher court which can call on experts chosen from many countries can be of great help to the local courts.

The legal expertise of the Sacred Rota, a pre-condition of its ability to help the local courts in the above-mentioned manner, has often been praised by popes.

However it is obvious to all that this function is running into various sorts of trouble at the moment. The main difficulty seems to be, on the one hand, the poor knowledge of Latin, the language with which the court operates and records its proceedings in large tomes, and on the other hand, the fact that collections of local judgments are published in various other countries. Often only these local legal books are read, because they are printed in a language which is understood, with the resulting danger that the level of legal knowledge decreases and that the law becomes localised with the same mistakes constantly repeated without recourse to a broader view. Furthermore different applications of the law in particular cases (apart from the differences necessarily arising from different circumstances) gives rise to the danger of 'migration'—the application for a hearing of a particular case in the country where the desired solution is most likely to be given, which inevitably causes scandal.

To overcome this problem, it would probably be a good idea to publish the legal tomes of the Sacred Rota in shorter form, omitting the less important and the less relevant parts. And of course these extracts could also be published in various modern languages.

This more rigourous selection might also do away with the reasons for publishing the court's proceedings only every ten years, so that books recording more recent decisions would be available more quickly.

Of course this work would have to be done by carefully chosen experts from various countries and cultures.

2. THE SUPREME COURT OF THE APOSTOLIC SIGNATURA

Unlike the Sacred Rota, the Apostolic Signatura is a department which was subjected to sweeping reforms in the Constitution *Regimini Ecclesiae Universae*. This has given it a special importance in the Church's bureaucracy and made it an object of increasing interest in recent canonistic literature because of the new duties assigned to it. Two of these are of particular importance:

1. *Its watchdog function*[2] This function is not simply the supervision of courts, but a duty to watch over the *fair administration of justice*. Thus its function is not just a controlling one, but includes the duty to make sure that justice is really done. The Apostolic Signatura has made clear that it wants to fulful this duty by offering brotherly help to courts in their service for the good of souls.[3]

These functions operate in various ways:

The Apostolic Signatura examines the annual and five-yearly records sent to it by the individual courts, in order to supervise the actual functioning of the administration of justice (necessary in order to fulfil its watchdog role).

If sometimes it discovers procedural irregularities or substantial defects in the verdicts of individual courts, it merely intervenes by sending its own observations to the court and begging it to take them into consideration.

It may also be appealed to when, with good reason, a court is accused of serious mishandling of the law or denial of the defendant's rights in a particular case. Then, if after examining the matter it decides that these grave accusations are well founded, it usually refers the case for re-trial or for the quashing of the verdict to the Sacred Rota. In certain cases the pope himself has referred a case to the Sacred Rota. The Apostolic Signatura follows a similar procedure when it finds serious irregularities in verdicts and communicates its opinions of them to the appropriate civil courts.

In certain cases the pope himself has taken charge of cases which he considered ought to be studied in greater depth by the cardinals. These cases have been of various kinds.[4]

If examination of a case shows the need to improve certain aspects of the judicial functioning in a particular country, the pope sends his own observations to the appropriate Episcopal Conference, together with specific proposals.

Although it is not the job of the Apostolic Signatura to publish advice or interpretations of the law, it will reply to the many requests sent by individual courts, with the opinion of one of its experts in the form of private advice. However it sometimes gives more forceful replies, and a particularly important recent case of this was its declaration of the competence of the US courts[5] to deal with a problem which gave rise to insoluble conflicts until it was resolved.

In its watchdog capacity, in many simple cases, the Apostolic Signatura declares a marriage to be null as an administrative measure, when such a case cannot be satisfactorily solved by the appropriate court.[6]

In many cases, in order to facilitate the administration of justice, it allows the adjournment of a trial (Pontifical Commissions).

Its supervision of the proper administration of justice includes the task of setting up inter-diocesan courts.[7] It has so far succeeded in doing this in fifty countries.

The pope has given the Apostolic Signatura certain facilities to enable it to fulfil its functions and help courts and petitioners in other ways: e.g., to give dispensations from the laws of procedure in particular cases; to amend null and void judicial pronouncements; to allow bishops to nominate a layman as counsel for the defence (in a contested nullity case) or 'x' as 'promoter of justice',[8] etc.

2. The other function of the Apostolic Signatura, given to it by the reform of the Roman curia, concerns *trials contesting the Church bureaucracy*. This is intended to give the faithful better protection against the working of the Church bureaucracy.

The introduction of such trials is an important innovation in the functioning of canon law. It is a definite improvement on the procedure laid down in the Code which only allowed recourse to a hierarchically higher administrative body (can. 1601).

The Apostolic Signatura has had to draw up rules for the conduct of such trials. Up till now there have been about 200 appeals made to the Apostolic Signatura against the Church bureaucracy, even though many of these have been turned down initially because of the lack of rules for procedure established by law.

However this is only a first step. The Apostolic Signatura is not an adequate body to give proper protection to private persons in all the conflicts that arise between them and the Church bureaucracy. So the Commission for the revision of the Code envisages the setting up of administrative courts of various kinds at various levels.[9] As we know in some countries there have already been discussions and experiments with such courts.

Translated by Dinah Livingstone

Notes

1. See I. Gordon 'De nimia processum matrimonialium duratione' *Periodica* 58 (1969) pp. 500-3.

2. *Regimini Ecclesiae Universae,* art. 105.

3. Circular *Inter cetera* 28.12.1970. nn. 5-6. (see also the introduction which speaks of 'munus *consulendi* rectae administrationi iustitiae') in AAS 63 (1971) pp. 480-6.

4. See *Periodica* 60 (1971) pp. 306-8; 62 (1973) pp. 11-38, 567-80; 66 (1977) pp. 297-325; *Apollinaris* 48 (1975) pp. 19-28; 49 (1976) pp. 19-29.

5. *Communicationes* 10 (1978) pp. 20-2.

6. See Z. Grocholewski 'La facolta del congresso della Signatura Apostolica di emettere dichiarazioni di nullità di matrimonio in via amministrativa, *Investigationes Theologico-Canonicae* (Rome 1978) pp. 211-32.

7. *Inter cetera,* op. cit. see AAS 63 (1971) p. 480. See also the *Norms* laid down for the Apostolic Signatura, *ibid.,* pp. 486-92.

8. See Z. Grocholewski 'Nominatio laicorum ad munus promotoris iustitiae et defensoris vinculi in recentissima praxi' *Periodica* 66 (1977) pp. 271-95.

9. See *Communicationes* 1 (1969) 82-3; 2 (1970) 191-4; 4 (1972) 35-8; 5 (1973) 235-43.

Emma Cavallaro

Women in the Roman Curia

IT IS at one and the same time very easy and very difficult to talk about the presence of women in the Roman curia. As a matter of fact, one could simply present the reader with the small numbers of women involved. But it might be more useful to attempt to reflect on the matter, and to look into the future. There are not many women working in the curia: their presence amounts to less than five per cent. There are no women, for example in the following departments: the Congregation for the Sacraments and Divine Worship, the Congregation for Saints' Causes, the Commission for the Revision of the Code of Canon Law, the Commission for the Interpretation of the Decrees of Vatican II, the Commission for Social Communications, and the International Theological Commission. Among those women who do work in the curia, it is possible to identify the religious and the handful of married women, but as far as the remainder are concerned, it is always difficult to know how many belong to secular institutes—though the majority in fact do—simply because the institutes concerned are those where secrecy is still observed. From the geographical point of view, the European presence is quite representative, possibly with the emphasis on Spain and Italy, but it is important to recognise the complete absence of representation where other continents are concerned.

The essential thing is to ask oneself what those women who are present in the curia actually do. Their duties are generally at the administrative level, requiring a combination of administrative ability and intelligence, and most of them are typists and secretaries. In view of the present character of the curia, it is difficult to imagine a greater and better 'utilisation' of the gifts of the women, and of what they have to contribute—it is known for a fact that only ordained persons can exercise jurisdiction in the various congregations. It is, however, necessary to establish what exactly constitutes an exercise of jurisdiction—on close analysis it would seem that such exercises are relatively few and far between. It will, perhaps, be enough to recall, for example, that with the *motu proprio* December 10 1976, the Council for the Laity, which was established on an experimental basis on January 6 1967, 'was given stable and definitive form' as a Vatican department assuming the title Pontifical Council for the Laity, and by the same token there were no longer any lay people among its principal officers, whereas during the experimental period there were two of them, one of them a woman, who served as vice-secretaries. In fact the women who work in the curia scarcely ever have an opportunity to contribute directly the fruits of their thought and reflection. If they are religious they can always hope that their contribution, which is not sought out in the curia, may be channelled through the national or international bodies to which they belong and which are sometimes asked for their opinions.

Obviously the question of the presence of women in the curia is part of the wider question of the presence of lay people in general, and in fact one frequently asks oneself whether certain offices or functions might not be more suitably filled by lay people than by priests. It is also legitimate to ask whether the latter can really fulfill their priestly vocation in working for the curia, even taking into account the fact that some pastoral activity is obligatory. Reflection along these lines could have far-reaching consequences, especially in view of the difficulties faced by the clergy in so many parts of the world, and of the scarcity of their numbers. What is more, if in the past it was more difficult to find qualified lay people, today this is increasingly less of a problem, partly on account of the growing number of lay people who are studying theology.

It remains true to say, however, that even where more room has been made for women, discrimination still exists. In the section for religious in the Congregation for Religious and Secular Institutes, we find a male religious with the title of 'head of department' and a female religious who, although her status is the same as his, is said to be in charge of the Office for Affairs Relating to the Chapters and Constitutions of Religious Institutes of Women'. The question of a different way of sharing out the work is certainly important and should be discussed, but it seems this will have to wait until time can be spared for it. However, in more recent years other possibilities have emerged and yet others could well do so, in the form of committees and commissions entrusted with specific tasks. In these cases there is no doubt that new and more flexible methods of work could be tried out, not least because if the past is anything to go by, their constitutive documents often leave ample room for freedom and experimentation, present and future.

This is another very important consideration. A 'good pastor', one who works well in his diocese, who, through the way he governs or in his pastoral work, wins the affection and collaboration of every sector of the people of God and who has succeeded in establishing genuine participation and collaboration, can only be spared with difficulty from his diocese or from his work. How many episcopal conferences can afford to relinquish effective, trained individuals who are already deeply involved in pastoral work? So, without wishing to judge anyone and always recognising the existence of praiseworthy exceptons, one can say that it is this absence of true pastors which determines what is generally defined as the 'curial mentality', and it is this mentality together with the restricting bureaucratic moralism that goes with it, that one unfortunately meets with even at the committee and commission level. It is thus that some of the best opportunities are in fact lost, ideas born of someone's intelligent intuition which could mean progress for the Church in the matter of studies, reflection and deepening of insight, leading on to new forms of pastoral practice. If this is in fact to take place, what is essential is a courageous respect for the liberty of the children of God, which, if it truly is such takes nothing away from fidelity but rather invests it with its true significance. When they are entrusted to timid men who are incapable of living or of facing the future with joy, even the best insights are unproductive and in fact exclude every possibility of growth. Many lay people have come up against this obstacle, and in particular many women, who still look with some sadness on their own experience, profoundly aware of the fact that they have not succeeded in getting the Church to take any significant step forward in the examination of those problems which call her in question today and challenge her missionary identity.

Such considerations as these demonstrate just how urgent it is that the opportunities for work and collaboration within the various departments of the curia should be differently organised. One needs only to reflect on the high number of consultors who, at least once a year, come from all over the world to take part in the plenary meetings. The criteria for their nomination are frequently related to the question of geographical representation, and it is particularly difficult to find women theologians, jurists and economists—one need only recall the fact that in the Study Commission on Women in Society and in the Church, the above-mentioned functions were, with one exception, entrusted to men. But quite apart from this consideration, the question remains how much someone can contribute effectively to the general work of an organisation by taking part in a meeting once a year. At the best there might be some preparatory work, but how significant and how representative will it be? And represenative of whom and of what kind of experience? Often enough the people involved are those favoured by the nunciatures in the countries they come from, and one hears of cases in which the episcopal conference in question has not been consulted, and in which, had it been so, would never have given its consent. The time has really come for us to ask whether we ought not to be looking for new, less formalistic and more efficient, patterns and methods of work. We need, for example, to ask whether it is more important to bring together people of different nationality, race and colour, or should we be making the local churches genuinely responsible, so that they can promote reflection and examination in depth of the themes in question? The results might usefully filter through to bodies that are more flexible and able to attend to the real problems of daily life, a life which only too often seems to be carried on at one or two removes from the curia, without impinging on it at all. Eventually, if the need is felt for consultations involving geographical representation, one might have recourse to the type of international consultation of the laity which took place in Rome in 1975. Among the recommendations presented to the 1974 synod of bishops by the Study Commission on Women in Society and in the Church was one to the effect that the participation of women 'in posts involving effective and recognised responsibility' should be encouraged. One may hope that this recommendation has had some results in the various local churches, but there can be no doubt that at the curial level it has fallen on deaf ears.

If this is a serious matter and unjust as far as women themselves are concerned, it is much more so for the Church as a whole, which is passing up the opportunity to realise a genuine experience of communion and depriving itself of a contribution and a collaborative effort, the possibilities and potential of which are unknown to it. If it is true that the Church is 'at one and the same time holy and ever in need of purification', it is also true that it will be difficult for her to achieve authentic renewal of the quality of her life unless she examines more courageously her attitudes to the participation of women and the possibility of creating conditions which would allow each individual to realise the divine plan in his regard, his own Christian vocation which derives not from sex but from the Holy Spirit.

Translated by Sarah Fawcett

Lamberto de Echeverría

The Pope's Representatives

I SHALL try to answer two questions in the course of this article:

1. Can we assess the existence and function of papal representatives in 1979 as worthless, satisfactory, desirable or even excellent?
2. What currently valid arguments would support such an assessment?

1. AN ASSESSMENT OF THIS INSTITUTION

I have already made an assessment of this institution at the strictly technical level[1] and would now like to do so at the pastoral level. I would like to pose the question whether these institutions which represent the pope say, or ought to say, anything to the Catholic who is interested in the life of the Church and the effective application of the Council; who is concerned about the present and future of the Church and who does not go by superficial impressions but is well informed and thinks.

The latest edition of the *Annuario Pontificio*[2] contains eighteen packed pages which list the various institutions representing the Holy See all over the world. This world-wide network of different bodies ranges from the diplomatic to the purely religious institution, and their remit may be exclusive to one country or may include several countries. This phenomenon of religious sociology and international organisation is as unique as the Church itself, which these various bodies represent.

But what is the theoretical function of these representative bodies? Responding to the wishes of the Council, Pope Paul VI systematically organised the activity of these institutions in his Motu Proprio of June 24 1969, *Sollicitudo omnium ecclesiarum*. This is a fundamental document and will be a frequent point of reference in this article.[3] The most important section is the fourth one which states:

56

'1. The primary and specific purpose of the mission of the pope's representative is to strengthen the bonds between the Holy See and local churches and make them more effective.
2. He also voices the pope's concern for the welfare of the country in which he is exercising this mission; he has a special obligation to work zealously for peace, progress and co-operation between peoples to improve the spiritual, moral and material well-being of the whole human family.
3. In co-operation with local Bishops, the papal representative has the duty of protecting the interests of the Church and the Holy See before the civil authorities of the place where he is exercising his office. This work is also part of the remit of those papal legates who are not diplomats and so they should make it their concern to maintain friendly relations with local authorities.
4. As instructed by the competent authorities within the Holy See and in accord with the wishes of local hierarchies—especially with the Eastern Patriarchates—the papal representative, as the envoy of the supreme pastor of souls, will promote suitable contacts between the Catholic Church and other Christian communities and will encourage cordial relations with non-Christian religions.'

The profound change intended by the Council in the manner of understanding the work of pontifical representatives is self-evident. There is no need to go further back than the 1917 revision of the Code and compare what was said then with what is stated above. In order of importance, diplomacy comes after the work of maintaining close contact between the Holy See and local churches, and contributing to the welfare of the country. What is completely new is the work of relating with other religions, Christian or otherwise, as mentioned in No. 4 above. In the Motu Proprio, this basic description is completed by mention of the duty of providing information, participating in the appointment of bishops and in dealings with local hierarchies, relating with Episcopal Conferences and Religious Orders and taking part in international conferences and organisations.

My own contact with papal representatives both in Spain and abroad, throughout a long priestly life, has taught me that the practical application of this theoretical description shows up the complex nature of their work. They asked for information on legal matters, they enquired about the suitability of people for episcopal appointments and they sought information on publications and territorial re-organisation. This flow of information occasionally changed direction, both at home and abroad, where the papal legate was an acquaintance or had good reason for imparting information to me.

In addition, I once officially received a very severe reprimand for one article (which incidentally would have gone un-noticed today) and was given instructions about the publication of other articles by myself and others. The nunciature sought information about international meetings and conferences in order to appoint a suitable representative of the Holy See, who might attend and give an objective report on how things had gone. Therefore, even from the point of view of a provincial university lecturer, the nunciature is far from being merely representative and light-weight, because it asks for and provides information, because it censures and encourages and because it plays a part in the internal and external affairs of the local church. Sometimes the reasons for that kind of local intervention are immediately apparent; on other occasions, they do not become clear until many years later. As a newly ordained priest I was taken by the energy with which the nuncio fought the pro-German convictions of my own bishop who was following the current trend. It was not until much later that I was to learn about the very serious reasons why he adopted such an attitude; reasons which Spaniards, including the bishops, were totally unaware of, blinded as we were by official propaganda. How many of us even suspected what was happening to the Jews?[4]

Pontifical legations, therefore, constitute the most practical method of ensuring that in each local and national church there exists one person who is exceptionally well informed about the Holy See and the universal Church, and who can act independently of the local church though this may not exclude immunity from local pressure. There are few exceptions to the general rule that such a person will already have a wide experience of the diversity within the Church at local levels. Even at the risk of incurring disfavour, let me state that I believe we are dealing here with an institution which is doctrinally and practically justified, though capable of improvement and already in the process of reform.

This claim will inevitably cause argument. Papal representatives were not always accepted peacefully in the past. Local churches, to say nothing of Royal Households and governments, often resented the presence of a foreigner over whom they had no control and who often contradicted and curtailed their own authority. Today, criticism comes not just from people on the periphery of the Church or who are acting against it, but from within the Church itself—bishops who spoke out during the Second Vatican Council, and leading cardinals who have spoken out since the Council.[5]

Criticism is varied. Some believe that the institution itself was defective from its inception. Historically, it can be proved that today's nunciatures have political and economic origins because as sovereigns of a small European state, the popes became involved in international power-balancing and alliances, and needed collectors to amass wealth. The improvements of time have not entirely removed some of the original defects. But, is this a valid criticism in 1979, after the publication, for example, of documents about the activity of the Holy See during the Second World War? I also feel that relics of the old order, like reserved benefices and the need to petition purely formal dispensations, have disappeared in the post-Conciliar era.

Others think that what is at stake is ecclesiology itself. They feel that underlying the presence and activity of the pope's representatives is the concept that local churches are simply administrative divisions of the universal Church. This criticism, which can also be justified historically, was valid enough in the past and could be supported by arguments from the Code of Canon Law itself, but I believe that it has no credibility today, not just in the light of the Motu Proprio, *Sollicitudo onmium ecclesiarum,* but for practical reasons based on the new importance of Episcopal Conferences and the strengthening of the role of the bishops after the Council.[6] The same ecclesiological argument would accuse the pope's representatives, especially in countries where the faith is still young, of being some kind of 'Superbishops' who stifle the initiative and activity of the local bishops. This danger, which has always existed and is mentioned in the Code itself (Canon 269, No. 1), is dealt with quite decisively in the Motu Proprio: '*Regarding the bishops who by divine mandate are responsible for the care of souls on each diocese*, the papal representative has *the duty of helping, advising, and working* readily and generously *with them, in a spirit of brotherly co-operation* and always respecting the exercise of their own jurisdiction' (No. VIII).

There are those who ask what is achieved by this interference in the religious activities of another country and why problems cannot be solved without recourse to diplomacy, an area of sharp practice and which the Church should obviously avoid. They suggest that local authorities should be left to their own devices and deal directly with their own local governments. But, the fact is that, despite its shortcomings, there is no substitute for diplomacy. Furthermore, local religious authorities are more liable to be biased and subjected to more pressures than the universal Church, and history shows that the intervention of those who have widened their experience in other countries and are well informed is to the advantage of the local church. Let these examples from Spain suffice: the nunciature put an end to the excesses of Spanish Integrism (and became a target of its anger), curbed the ecclesiastical despotism of Cardinal Segura, imposed some moderation on the pro-German tendencies of the Spanish bishops during the Second World War, and promoted the effective implementation of the Council to become the hope of those of us who wished to go that way.

Serious errors have been committed; for example, the politicking by Mgr. Antoniutti; but this only indicates that a certain line of action has gone awry, not that the operation was badly planned in its entirety.[7]

Lastly, there are purely practical objections. Without any ulterior motives, some object to the ostentation, luxury and life-style of papal delegations. They object to the fact that personnel is recruited from a very limited area (for centuries most of these have been Italians) and that their formation is bureaucratic rather than pastoral, with the result that the popular image of the pope's representatives is of a group of Italians, installed in key positions, who interfere in the activities of the local churches and exercise some control over them. The same critics raise doubts about whether the man-power and money expended on this kind of operation is proportionate to the results. The measures which have already been taken prove that these criticisms were justified. Personnel is selected on a wider international basis; they are encouraged to pursue more pastoral work and widen the area of their work so that the results obtained may be in proportion to the effort deployed.[8]

A brief reply to the practical objection might include a dictum from insurance advertising: 'Insurance is expensive only before a mishap'! But surely diplomacy is worth all the effort if it can avert disaster in one solitary situation of real conflict. And it is not just one but many such conflicts that have been defused by diplomacy both in the past and in our own time.[9]

2. DOCTRINAL AND PRACTICAL FOUNDATIONS

If we accept the doctrine of the primacy of the Roman Pontiff as defined by the First Vatican Council (see Canon 218), the service of the universal Church demands that the pope should be somehow present in an adequate form everywhere on earth, and be aware of the state of each local church. This is because Jesus Christ 'when he gave his Vicar the power of the keys, and made him the foundation stone of his Church, also gave him the mandate to "strengthen his brethren" which is achieved not only by guiding them and keeping them united in his name, but also by encouraging them and comforting them through his words, and to a certain extent, by his presence'.[10] This is achieved by the journeys undertaken by the pope, by visits from bishops, especially the 'ad limina' visit and by means of the representatives whom the pope sends to the local churches. This is the principal reason for the existence of the institution under review.

Furthermore, although not a political but a religious society, the

Church 'finds herself involved with States in both internal and external relations; since it has been established by Christ as a visible society—sharing the same territory as states—its concern embraces the same people under various aspects and it makes use of the same material goods and institutions as the state'.[11] Maintaining the Church's presence in the international order has become even more urgent in the modern world. One example will suffice. After Nazi Germany declared war on the Soviet Union during the course of the last war, the influence of the Apostolic Delegate over the bishops of the United States was of crucial importance. Germany's attempt to present this war as a crusade failed completely, and the North American bishops' positive reaction influenced the course of the war in a way which would not have been possible if their decisions had been taken without the delegate's intervention. But, anecdotes apart, if the current re-awakening of nationalism is bad in itself, surely it will prove fatal as a feature of the Church? The nationalist tendency to create frontiers between local churches has to be balanced by the inter-nationalism of pontifical delegations.[12] Let us not forget that despite their many advantages, Episcopal Conferences cannot avoid nationalist tendencies for which, as in other aspects, the pope's representatives can provide a counter-weight. These two doctrinal arguments are supported and at the same time limited by *practical considerations*. They are *supported* by the successes already achieved by pontifical representatives in many fields ranging from the strictly religious (e.g., their effectiveness in maintaining communications with the Holy See during the Second World War or their co-operation in the establishment of some Episcopal Conferences) to the political (e.g., the recent case in which the threat of war between Chile and Argentina was defused by a papal intermediary). They are *limited* by the fact that contact with reality often reduces the high purposes of doctrinal and juridical statements which are consequently in need of constant revision.

It should be noted that this kind of *modification* is a continuous process. The diplomatic service, which previously implied progress through a series of palatial surroundings, today may involve living austerely for many years in under-developed countries where the climate and milieu can be difficult.[13] A deepening spirituality and a widening of international awareness along with an increasing pastoral sensitivity are, today, easily recognisable aspects of the pontifical diplomat's work. Episcopal Conferences provide an obvious counter-weight to previous abuses because dealing with bishops who are united by a common purpose is quite different from dealing with them in isolation. Diplomatic secrecy which caused local bishops to be taken unawares by agreements and territorial changes arranged without their knowledge has been modified to the extent that today Episcopal Conferences are well informed about

Church-State negotiations. The impact of the Council has been far-reaching, and although there still remains a great deal to be done there is no doubt that in this area the future is very hopeful indeed.

Translated by John A. Macdonald

Notes

1. 'Legados del Romano Pontifice', *Enciclopedia jurídica Seix* Vol. 14 (Barcelona 1971) pp. 841-865; *Cómo está Organizada Hoy la Iglesia* (Madrid 1974) pp. 21-25.

2. pp. 1108-1126 of the 1978 edition.

3. Official Latin text in A.A.S. Vol. 61 (1969) pp. 473-484. I have written a commentary on it in *Revista Española de Derecho Canónico* 24, (1970) pp. 573-636. Another basic text for understanding the position of the Holy See is the letter of the Secretary of State, Cardinal Jacobini, to the nuncio in Madrid, dated April 15 1885, published in A.A.S. Vol. 17 (1884) pp. 561-569 (the discrepancy in the dates is due to the fact that the 1884 part of A.A.S. appeared very late).

4. Several dispatches from the nuncio, Gaetano Cicognani, published in *Actes et Documents du Saint Siège relatifs à la Seconde Guerre Mondiale* (Vatican City 1970-75), refer to his efforts to make the Spanish bishops aware of the dangers of Nazi Germany. Documents about the Holy See's opposition to the *Spiritual and Cultural Co-operation Treaty between Spain and Germany* of January 24 1939, which prevented this agreement being ratified, have just been edited and published: A. Marquina, 'La Iglesia española y los planes culturales alemanes para España', *Razón y Fe* No. 199 (1979) pp. 354-370.

5. I refer to the unfortunate statements made by Cardinal Suenens to José de Broucker in 'L'unité de l'église', *Informations Catholiques Internationales* 15 (1969), a supplement to number 336, especially the section entitled 'Le statut et la mission du Nonce' pp. XIII-XV. The claims of all parties in this polemic were collected, systematically arranged and studied by Mgr. Montini, then depute Secretary of State and the future Paul VI on April 25 1951 in a discourse published in I. Cardinale *Le Saint-Siège et la Diplomatie* (Paris 1962) in which he presents his own arguments as well. Number 9 of the Conciliar Decree *Christus Dominus* expressed the desires of the Fathers of the Council that 'in view of the pastoral role proper to bishops, the functions of the legates of the Roman Pontiff should be more precisely determined'.

6. See the papers by Bonet Muixi, Lodos Vilariño, Echevarría and Bidagor on different aspects of the question in *La Función Pastoral de los Obispos* (Salamanca 1967) and also J. Sanchez y Sanchez *Dinámica Jurídica posconciliar* (Salamanca 1969).

7. The activities of the nunciature vis-à-vis integrism have been studied by R. M. Sanz de Diego, for example see 'Una aclaración sobre los origines del integrismo: la peregrinación de 1882', *Estudios Eclesiasticos* 52 (1977) pp. 91-122, and the letter of Cardinal Jacobini referred to above in Note 3. Parts of this letter have been selectively edited by Postius, *El Código de Derecho Canónico Aplicado a España* 5th edition (Madrid 1927), No. 363. Cardinal Segura resigned as Archbishop of Seville on the last day of the time allotted him to lift certain arbitrarily imposed censures. Political implications have been attributed to this incident

which was a matter of internal discipline in the Church and which was honourably conducted by all parties: a seriously tendentious version is that of R. Garriga *El Cardenal Segura y el Nacional-Catolicismo* (Barcelona 1977) p. 313. On attitudes during the Second World War, see Note 4 above. The work of the nunciature in favour of the establishment of a reasonable democracy during the Second Republic is documented in two volumes by Arxiú Vidal i Barraquer *Esglesia i Estat Durant la Segona Republica Espayola* (Monsterrat 1975) and a biased approach appears in the pamphlet by Persiles (R. Sanchez Mazas) *España-Vaticano* (Madrid 1932). The best example of Mgr. Antoniutti's interventions is his discourse to participants in the Fourth World Congress of the Catholic Press held at Comillas in 1960. The *Actas* of the Congress were published by the Spanish National Committee of the Catholic Press in 1961.

8. Details about the internationalisation of the Vatican's Diplomatic Corps appear in my own Commentary to the Motu Proprio referred to in Note 3 above, p. 607.

9. See for example, the third volume (in two sections) of *Actes et Documents* . . . (referred to in Note 4), for the difference between countries which rightly or wrongly maintained a papal legation and those which, like Poland and the Baltic States, were deprived of it.

10. See paragraph 1 of the Introduction to the Motu Proprio *Sollicitudo Omnium Ecclesiarum*; and also the Introduction to the Decree *Ad Romanam Ecclesiam* of June 29 1975 on the *ad limina* visit, and my own Commentary in *Revista Española* de *Derecho Canónico* No. 32 (1976) pp. 359-419, especially pp. 382-383.

11. Pius XII, *Discorsi e Radiomessagei di Sua Santità* Vol. 13 p. 426.

12. I refer to the ever-increasing demand, reflected even in some concordats, for a bishop to belong to the same nation, region and even the diocese over which he is to govern. An absurd tendency, contrary to Church history and about which I wrote at the time of the election of Pope John Paul II: 'The pope emphasises the fact that he is non-Italian . . . and when I heard this, I was reminded of an article I read a few days ago in the French newspaper *La Croix*. The author was explaining why it had been impossible to elect a non-Italian pope. He complained that nationalism was still too rampant in our universal Church. Underlying the article was a recall of the time when a Yugoslavian like Saint Martin could become a great Bishop of Tours in the same way as Saint Toribio of Mogrovejo could become the Apostle of South America and the organiser of its ecclesiastical hierarchy. The article also reminded me that my own Diocese of Salamanca was restored by a French bishop and had an outstanding Portuguese bishop.' See *La Religión* (Caracus) November 5 1978 p. 4.

13. Has sufficient thought been given to what it means to a normal person to be uprooted from his own country to spend his life going from one country to another? To be deprived of genuine friendship in an area where relations are liable to be tainted by selfishness and ambition? To have to live in a very enclosed community and be deprived of freedom, knowing that information which is passed on can have a decisive influence on his future? Perhaps the popular image is very far removed from the truth and that these appointments are very demanding especially for those who have no special aptitudes for that kind of life.

Norbert Greinacher

Lack of Communication between Leadership and Base in the Church

THE *'Joint Synod of Dioceses in the Federal Republic of Germany'* and its *Relation to the Roman Curia.*

The Joint Synod was held in Würzburg in eight sessions between 1971 and 1975. Around 70 bishops, 130 priests and religious and 140 lay people took part in it. The eighteen resolutions of the plenary session and the six working papers from the special commissions have since been published in an official collected edition.[1] The resolutions were published in the official newspapers of all the dioceses.[2] Many full-time and part-time functionaries of the Church invested a great deal of time and energy in this synod. The work of the synod also consumed considerable financial resources. Was this expense worth while? Above all, did it succeed in giving expression to the problems, sufferings and difficulties of individual members of the Church and individual parishes and providing a solution for them? Were the central pastoral problems of the Catholic Church in West Germany reported to the Roman curia? Did the Roman curia come to the aid of the West German Church in a subsidiary way?

1. DISALLOWED 'VOTA'

In the case of three important problems of pastoral practice there was no formal submission (*votum*) to the Roman curia because the German Bishops' Conference did not allow a preliminary resolution to be put at the synod, a power given them by the procedural rules. On April 13 1972 the Bishops' Conference decided that the question of the admission of married men to the priesthood should be excluded from the subjects for discussion. This decision provoked a crisis of confidence in the synod, and there was a risk of the temporary withdrawal of about a third of the members. However, the relevant resolution of the synod eventually included the following statement: 'It is therefore generally recognised that extraordinary pastoral emergencies may require the ordination of men who have proved themselves in their marriages and professions.'[3]

Again in the case of two further matters, relating to the pastoral care of the married, the German Bishops' Conference prevented the moving of a resolution about a submission to Rome. In the draft produced by special commission IV the pope was to be asked 'to examine, with the synod of bishops, whether, in the Gospel spirit of freedom, with reference to the Matthaean unchastity clause (Matt 5:32; 19:9) and the Pauline decision (I Cor 7:12-16), and in view of the practice of the Eastern Church, existing canon law may be altered and those of the faithful who have been left alone despite their readiness for reconciliation may be given the possibility of another marriage in the Church'.[4] The question raised was thus the one also discussed at the Council of Trent, whether adultery could be grounds for divorce. In the other disallowed submission Rome would have been asked whether 'civil marriages of Catholics who, in spite of all pastoral efforts, do not have, or do not want to have, any contact with the Church may be regarded as marriages, which, while not attaining the sacramental dimension, in their personal and legal dimension are in a special way ordered towards it.'[5] The disallowing of this submission thus again blocked an escape from a situation of great difficulty for all concerned.

2. THE SUBMISSIONS TO THE ROMAN CURIA

In all the synod passed nineteen submissions (not sixteen, as often reported) which were to be put to the Roman curia.[6] They experienced different fates.

The submission on the participation of the laity in preaching (No. 1) was given a favourable answer (though with very restrictive conditions), while the synod was still in progress, in the rescript of the Congregation for the Clergy dated November 20 1973 and the guidelines issued by the meeting of the German Bishops' Conference of March 3-7 1974.

Another submission (No. 2), asked for the right to organise a Joint Synod every ten years. The secretariat of the German Bishops' Conference claims that it was accepted, but this cannot be so. The relevant letter of the apostolic nuncio, dated November 18 1976, stresses explicitly that the Holy See regards the Joint Synod, 'permitted at the time as an experiment', as concluded.[7] In the case of similar institutions at national level either the existing regulations of the code of canon law or those prepared by the papal commission for the reform of canon law must be followed. 'In addition it is always possible to use other forms of meeting which—without possessing the binding character of a synod—allow the various representatives of the local churches to participate in the study of their problems. The Holy See reserves the right to issue general regulations for this type of meeting, which may not be called either a "synod" or a "council".' In other words, there will not be another Joint Synod, even though its terms of reference already left it only very limited scope. How the secretariat of the German Bishops' Conference can take this as a confirmation of the future of the Joint Synod is incomprehensible.

Submissions 3-7 were also rejected in practice. Submission 3, asking for the introduction of additional eucharistic prayers for young people was felt by the Vatican Congregation for the Liturgy and the Sacraments to be 'not appropriate'. On submission 4, that bishops should be authorised to delegate priests to administer confirmation, the Vatican secretariat of state stated that the apostolic see was unwilling to depart from the principle that the administering of confirmation was a specific responsibility of the local bishop. Also rejected was submission 5, asking that difference of denomination should no longer be a bar to marriage. In a sixth submission the synod asked the bishops 'to use all legitimate means to give separated Christians, if they so wish, access to the eucharist'.[8] Although this had the status of a submission of the synod, the president of the German Bishops' Conference did not forward this request until October 8 1976, and then merely as an 'inquiry' to the Secretariat for Christian Unity. From the secretariat, on May 5 1977, came the reply that there was no possibility of going beyond the cases provided for in the relevant instruction of the secretariat for unity. The synod's submission 7, on the admission of divorced and remarried Catholics to the sacraments, was also transformed by the German Bishops' Conference into an inquiry, dated April 20 1976, to the prefect for the Congregation for the Faith. Although a definitive answer has still not been given, the secretariat of the German Bishops' Conference expressed the, certainly correct, view that 'in the present state of the discussion there is no sign that an alteration of the existing rules can be expected.'[9]

There has certainly been no decision so far on the synod's request (No. 8) that a 'system of diocesan arbitration agencies and administrative courts' should be set up. This request is on the whole very welcome, since it would give members of the Church who feel that they have been unjustly treated by Church officials the right either to ask for arbitration or to submit a complaint under an administrative code. The German

Bishops' Conference had asked the secretariat of state to set up this system either by local regulations under the Roman outline law *De procedura administrativa* or, if work on this law was still likely to take some time, to empower the German Bishops' Conference to establish the system as a model for a local church. After repeated inquiries the prefect of the papal commission for the reform of canon law replied on July 3 1978, that the outline regulations were ready and were waiting for the pope's approval.

Submissions 9-19 have been passed to the competent Roman courts. According to a letter of November 18 1976, from the apostolic nuncio, they are to be taken into account in the revision of the code of canon law. The submissions made the following proposals:

9. Emotional maturity, and the absence of psychological pressures, etc. should be treated as necessary conditions for a valid marriage.

10. A Church marriage after the dissolution of a civil marriage should be allowed only under certain conditions.

11. Illegitimate children should have equal status in law with legitimate children.

12. It should be possible to appoint women as lectors and acolytes.

13. Women should have equality in canon law.

14. The minimum age for married permanent deacons should be reduced from thirty-five to thirty.

15. Permant deacons should be allowed to remarry after the death of their wives.

16. It should be possible for deacons who originally wanted to be priests to marry and continue to work as deacons.

17. Women should be ordained as deacons.

18. Laicised priests should be given all the rights of a lay person.

19. The period of office of a Council of Priests should not end with the death of the bishop.

Herder-Korrespondenz made the following comment on the treatment of the submissions by the Roman curia: 'The fate of the submissions—the short shrift generally given them by Rome, the Bishops' Conference's underestimate of their value as a publicity weapon—thus remains a proof that the hope of a "synodal style" of dealing with each other having been learnt in the Church during the Würzburg years was deceptive. How are the faithful supposed to form an "orthodox" judgment on these matters when they are not even allowed to know how they are discussed between the bishops and Rome? None of this unfortunately gives any sign of the "Church of hope" so much talked about in the past year.'[10]

3. ASSESSMENT

Let us go back to our original question. Were the central pastoral problems of the West German Church brought nearer to a solution as a result of the Joint Synod?

We may note first, on the positive side, that laity, priests and bishops worked, discussed, argued and celebrated the eucharist together for almost five years in the special commissions and the plenary sessions. Such a process of communication, and such a forum, has never been seen before in German Catholicism—and is unfortunately unlikely to be seen again in a hurry. Nor should the fact be ignored that the Joint Synod passed some very good final documents, such as 'The Teaching of Religion in Schools', 'Aims and Responsibilities of the Church's Youth Work', 'The Church and the Workers'. Taken as a whole, however, the synod cannot be said to have identified with the needs, concerns and difficulties of the members of the Catholic Church in West Germany. Measured by the criterion laid down by the Second Vatican Council's Constitution on the Church in the Modern World, that the Church should make its own 'the joys and the hopes, the griefs and the anxieties of the men of this age, especially those who are poor or in any way afflicted', the Joint Synod was largely a failure. It largely ignored the feelings and problems of the public both inside and outside the Church.

Hans Küng, at an ecumenical service in Tübingen on November 30 1975, rightly complained that the Joint Synod had disappointed those who had placed their hopes on it: the hopes of married people that there would at last be an unqualified acceptance of birth control, the hopes of the divorced who want to take part once more in the celebration of the eucharist, the hopes of theological students who feel called to the parochial ministry but not to celibacy, the hopes of the priests who have had to give up their office because of a lawful marriage, the hopes of the parishes which are being deprived of their priests mainly because of the law of celibacy, the hopes of the clergy and laity who are looking for a voice and a democratic procedure in the selection of their bishops, the hopes of all the individuals and communities who desire at last a mutual recognition of Church ministries and an open eucharistic communion.[11]

These and other problems of ordinary Catholics were not discussed because they were caught in a double filter. On the one hand, the rules of the Joint Synod and the method of appointment or election of its members made impossible the genuine representation of the laity and unrestricted freedom of discussion and decision. On the other hand, the decisions that were taken in spite of these restrictions were either not reported back to the base or bureaucratically stifled in the Roman curia.

The main problem, hiding behind these events, is ecclesiological in nature. If the Church continues to cling to a view of the Church as a hierarchical pyramid, these processes of filtering and deactivating any initiative from below can be repeated at any time, and is indeed logical and legitimate on the system's own terms. But if we start from a view of the Church such as the one embodied in the different strands of tradition in the New Testament, in which the individual ecclesial communities are the primary and essential point at which the Church comes into being, and all other institutions of the Church have the subsidiary function of enabling the Church to exist locally, a process such as the Joint Synod and its treatment by the Roman curia increasingly becomes a structural heresy.

What happened at the synod has a variety of consequences for the Catholic Church in West Germany. Among quite a number of members and even officials of the Church a paralysing resignation is spreading. Another group of Church members and officials is reacting to this dismal reaction on the part of the Roman curia to acute pastoral problems by ignoring existing Church laws in 'anticipatory obedience'. This applies, for example, to the use of non-approved eucharistic prayers, the reception of communion by non-Catholic Christians the admission of remarried divorced Catholics to the sacraments, to preaching by lay people (men and women) without restriction. This naturally also means that the Bishops' Conference and the Roman curia are themselves very effectively helping to undermine their own authority by either not reacting to pastoral problems or by reacting only dismissively or by imposing restrictions. The Church authorities are thus depriving themselves of the opportunity to inspire and stimulate pastoral movements at the base and give them worthwhile guidance.

Johann Baptist Hirscher, 130 years ago, in his day professor of theology at the University of Freiburg im Breisgau, proposed as subjects which should be discussed at a synod compulsory celibacy and the pastoral problem of marriages contracted only civilly and 'the attitude and activity of the clergy in relation to the present political parties'. He wrote at the time: 'A purely monarchical administration, of a diocese, for example, so completely contradicts the whole character of the present as to seem—in contrast to the constitutional and democratic life of the state—only possible and defensible if the whole of the intelligent section of the population were to abandon the Church or give itself over to the most complete religious indifference.'[12] Will Catholics in Germany and elsewhere have to wait so long again before solutions are found for their problems? The Church cannot afford to waste much more time.

Translated by Francis McDonagh

Notes

1. *Gemeinsame Synode der Bistümer in der Bundesrepublik Deutschland. Offizielle Gesamtausgabe,* vols I and II (Freiburg 1976 and 1977).

2. Press release of the secretariat of the German Bishops' Conference, January 17 1979.

3. *Gemeinsame Synode,* I, p. 628.

4. *Ibid.* p. 412.

5. *Ibid.*

6. See 'Die verdrängte Synode' ('The suppressed synod') *Herder-Korrespondenz* 31 (1977) pp. 537-540; Interim report on the submissions of the synod, *Herder-Korrespondenz* 33 (1979) pp. 64-68; Press release of the secretariat of the German Bishops' Conference, December 19 1978.

7. See the press release of December 19 1978.

8. *Gemeinsame Synode* I, p. 225.

9. Press release of December 19 1978.

10. Interim report on the submissions of the Joint Synod, *Herder-Korrespondenz* 33 (1979) pp. 64-66, quotation from p. 66.

11. *Paulinische Predigt* published by the Evangelische Studentengemeinde Tübingen (Stuttgart 1976) pp. 57-71.

12. Johann Baptist Hirscher *Die kirchlichen Zustände der Gegenwart* (Tübingen, 3rd ed. 1849).

Hansjakob Stehle

Roman 'Centrality'—
An Asset in Eastern Europe?

'The diplomat of the Holy See is first and foremost a priest.'

Paul VI, April 24 1978

ONE OF the criticisms made, especially in Western Church circles, of the Vatican's *Ostpolitik* is the charge that the Roman curia takes too little account of the interests of the local churches. The curia, it is said, seeks agreements with Communist governments over the heads of local bishops and tends, out of ignorance of local conditions, to appoint bishops who do not have the confidence of the faithful. Indeed, the diplomatic activities of the Vatican in general are said to exemplify an over-emphasis on institutional guarantees.

Such charges are, often unknowingly, based on the mistaken assumption that the curia's *Ostpolitik* has only one behavioural pattern and is unable to distinguish between the very different situations— geographical, political, psychological and, not least, pastoral—in which the Church has been and still is placed in the countries of official atheism. In particular there is a tendency to forget that the Vatican *Ostpolitik*, which began in the middle of the 1960s, is aimed primarily at the removal of rubble. After the breakdown of the last direct negotiations between the Soviet Union and the Vatican (at the end of 1927),[1] the structures of the Church, first in the Soviet Union and later, after 1944, in most of the Eastern European states, were totally destroyed or largely paralysed by Stalin's ecclesiastical policy. The episcopates were either liquidated or decimated, but above all their links with Rome were broken.

The Stalinists (who understood the nature of the Roman Church much better than many present-day internal opponents of 'Roman centralism')

71

regarded this separation as particularly important, since the moral and institutional support embodied in the supra-national papacy and the world Church was an element which could make holes in the 'iron curtain' and give a voice to a Church which had been condemned to silence. Accordingly the Vatican, and especially its diplomatic service, was branded as a 'headquarters of agents of American imperialism'. This enabled its 'branches', the local Catholic churches, to be kept under constant suspicion as being 'agencies' hostile to the state. The eagerness with which Pius XII attached himself to the 'cold war' trend in international politics and—after short, discreet attempts—avoided any attempt at contact with the Communists in power in Eastern Europe made it easier to isolate Eastern European Catholicism. It is true that the pope nowhere himself recalled his diplomatic representatives, still in place after the Second World War in Prague, Budapest, Bucharest, Belgrade, Sofia and Tirana, but he did accept their expulsion with resignation.

There were, however, two significant exceptions within this general process.

1. In the GDR, whose territory had been governed by special conditions as the Soviet zone of Germany and had had an open Western frontier until 1961, the Catholic minority was able to secure an area of relative freedom and also direct contact with Rome through verbal agreements with the Soviet military administration and through a sort of 'customary right'. The Roman curia tacitly sanctioned this. To avoid endangering this status quo, which has no legal basis, Cardinal Bengsch of Berlin nevertheless prefers today to leave matters of ecclesiastical administration arising out of the complicated state of intra-German relations (such as the pastoral case for establishing new dioceses or the provision of legal guarantees for the existence of the Church) exclusively to the Roman curia. 'There is a lot of talk about Roman centralism, but there is a danger of the rise of a new national centralism', Bengsch said as long ago as the Roman episcopal synod of 1969. On the other hand the curia, in spite of Bengsch's discreet pressure, has hesitated to throw its central authority into the scale without first securing the public agreement of the West German bishops.

2. In Poland, very soon after 1945, special papal powers had given the episcopate, and especially its cardinal primate, an autonomy which (although envisaged in fact as an expedient for emergencies) became, in the hand of Poland's powerful Catholicism, an effective instrument— though it was never regarded by the Roman curia as being as extensive as it was interpreted by Cardinal Wyszynski. The primate made his first agreement with the Communist government as early as 1950. For the government this was a preliminary expression of confidence, but it did not

prevent the Polish Church from playing a key role in the country during the next thirty years—now militant, now conciliatory—without having to seek Roman approval at every stage.

However, when Hungary's bishops (under Archbishop Groesz) in 1950 made an agreement with the government on the Polish model— though from a position of extreme weakness—the Roman curia responded unhesitatingly, on orders from Pius XII, with a direct rebuke. Political agreements on the scale of a concordat, it was said, were a matter for the Holy See alone; especially when effects on the position of the Church in other countries might be expected, this exceeded the competence of the bishops.[2] What was at stake, however, was not just the canonical powers of the bishops, but the very existence of the episcopates. It was inevitable that a prelate like Cardinal Josef Mindzenty, who regarded himself as the political leader of his people and even refused, in the summer of 1956, to return from internment to his archbishop's residence because he refused to accept 'favours from Communists' (the Nagy government), would sooner or later come into conflict with the Roman curia. The alternative to the relative *modus vivendi* negotiated for the Hungarian Church over the years by papal diplomacy under Paul VI was a *status moriendi* which—in religious terms—had begun there long before the Communist take-over, in essence as early as the 'Josefist' period. It was no accident that one of the first acts of Eastern European policy of the Polish Pope, John Paul II, was the sending of extraordinary nuncio Poggi to Hungary—as 'an interpreter of our pastoral concern', in Pope Wojtyla's words.[3]

To speak for the restricted local churches—in the framework of such an interpretative role and not one of paternalism—is the main task of Vatican pastoral diplomacy wherever pastoral work is particularly threatened.[4]

In the Soviet Baltic republics, especially Lithuania, the Church has won a minimum of breathing space since contact with Rome was restored at the end of the 1950s and some bishops appointed who have been able once again to travel regularly to Rome. Constant attempts by the state apparatus to sow discord between the faithful, the bishops and the Roman curia only confirm the vital importance of the Roman connection, which has never been limited to questions of jurisdiction, but has extended even to the provision of bibles and breviaries.

In Czechoslovakia, too, the problem of 'collegiality' has only been possible since the time when there have once again been some bishops (ordained by the Vatican 'foreign minister' Archbishop Casaroli, himself in a sort of 'emergency operation' in 1973). Since the authorities have so far forbidden the setting up of a Czechoslovak bishops' conference and are also trying to play off faithful, bishops and Vatican against each other (even by official 'toleration' of Felix Davidek, a 'secret bishop' consecrated without Roman approval), the bishops themselves, and the Roman curia have been seeking the closest possible contact, especially through travel. Numerous face-to-face conversations (both in the Vatican and in Czechoslovakia) have enabled the curia in the last few years to obtain a more accurate picture of the situation of the Church in Czechoslovakia than its critics imagine, while the Czechoslovak bishops for their part (and not just those accepted by the government) feel that their problems are given more attention and understanding than is visible on the surface. This is true to an even greater extent of the position of the Catholic Church in Rumania, where, if the Vatican can do very little, the local episcopate can do nothing at all in the face of the government's firm opposition to giving the Roman Church a canonically acceptable status.

There was no easing at all of the situation of the Catholic diaspora in Bulgaria until the spectacular visit of President Shivkoff to the Vatican in 1975. With a stroke of his dictator's pen, Shivkoff even allowed an astounded curia a bishop (Dobranov), who had been secretly consecrated sixteen years previously and constantly obstructed by the authorities. From the position of such a man, the problems of 'Roman curial centralism' must seem rather abstract.

There can be no doubt that the words Cardinal Wyszynski addressed with critical boldness to Paul VI on November 13 1965, apply beyond Poland. The cardinal said, 'To assess our position from a distance is difficult. Everything that happens in the life of our Church must be assessed from the standpoint of our experience. . . . If there is one thing that hurts us, it is lack of understanding. . . .' But can the local criterion be always and everywhere that of the universal Church and its supranational interests? The Roman curia could leave the strong Polish Church to its own resources ('La Polania farà da se') as long as its *Ostpolitik* was stagnating or doomed to total failure. The interdependence of the situations of the Church in the different countries, which is partly a result of the co-ordination of Communist ecclesiastical policy in Eastern Europe, makes a central, if differentiated, model of pastoral policy towards Eastern Europe within the Roman curia—despite all the concern for the local churches—unavoidable.

This has become even clearer since the election of a Polish bishop as pope. No-one can imply that it is difficult or perhaps impossible for him to judge the situation 'from a distance'. While his acceptance of the 'collegiality' of bishops comes from his own experience, it has always been— long before he became pope—tied to the centrality of the Petrine office: 'The bishops' share in responsibility emphasises still more the unique responsibility vested in the pope, and in him alone, in which he cannot be replaced by anyone' (Wojtyla 1969). This does not exclude the delegation of practical decisions to bishops' conferences on a larger scale than hitherto, but in policy towards Eastern Europe a Polish pope especially operates within narrow limits. In the ecclesiastical policy of the Soviet colonial power, everything 'Catholic' has always—as in the Tsarist period—been identified with 'Polish'. Even if the Roman curia, its approach and its personnel, does not undergo any process of 'Polonisation', it must in future expect this 'prejudice' at every step in its Eastern European policy. On the other hand, it can turn this into an asset for the Church if John Paul II succeeds in making himself as credible as the peace-loving pope of a universal Church as he did as a Catholic patriot in his native country. In this context Roman 'centrality' could even acquire a new significance—one stretching beyond its current theological and administrative problems.

Translated by Francis McDonagh

Notes

1. See H. Stehle *The Eastern Politics of the Vatican 1917-1978* (Ohio University Press 1979).

2. Letter from under-secretary of state Mgr. Dell'Acqua to Groesz, October 9 1950 ('. . . notum est publicas definire ac moderari rationes, quae Ecclesiae cum variis intercedunt Nationibus ad Sedem spectare Apostolicam . . .'). Complete text in Stehle, op. cit.

3. In a letter of December 2 1978 to the Hungarian episcopate read in all the churches of Hungary (cf. *Uj Ember*).

4. See H. Stehle *Concilium* 105/1977 p. 76.

José Dammert Bellido

Local Churches and their Communication with the Roman Curia: A Peruvian Diocese

TO UNDERSTAND the relations of the Roman curia with a diocese in the Peruvian Andes we need to bear in mind the historical background. Under Spanish rule, direct relations between the bishops and the Holy See did not exist, because everything had to be done through the Council of the Indies in Madrid. Moreover the Spanish ecclesiastical structure could not easily be adapted to the new continent, because of distance and the new missionary situation in those strange lands. Slowly there evolved in practice an 'Indian' legal code. This had no real scientific basis because, on the one hand, theologians and canonists simply reproduced European treatises without studying the special conditions which arose out of the actual situation, and on the other hand the bishops had no time for academic reflection upon pastoral practice. Even at the present time no study of the subject exists, because such investigations as have been made have been concerned almost exclusively with the relations between Church and State.

During the Republic, the problems resulting from liberation—such as vacancies in episcopal sees, the reduction in the number of clergy resulting from the expulsion of Spaniards, and political difficulties in the way of Rome's recognition of the new states—led to the maintenance of the older ecclesiastical structures and an absence of communication with the Roman curia.

The liturgical and canonical reforms of the pontificate of St Pius X, furthered in some measure by the holding of the Plenary Latin American Council in 1899, sought to impose patterns of Church life worked out in and for other latitudes. Some of them were reiterated by Provincial Councils, Episcopal Assemblies and Diocesan Synods, without producing any impact on pastoral practice. I might mention the pressure to extend the use of the Gregorian chant and the setting up at parochial level of the Congregation of Christian Doctrine. Neither of these has had any influence whatever.

There are traditional juridical customs which remain outside general canonical legislation, such as the privilege granted to the President of the Republic of presenting candidates to the parishes (recognised by a Papal Bull in 1874). However, since the beginning of the twentieth century the bishops have by-passed this presentation by appointing men to parishes in the guise of priests-in-charge, although in ordinary usage they are designated parish priests and are given this title also in episcopal decrees. In fact a whole series of canonical regulations, such as the immovability of parish priests, does not apply, although the lecturers in the seminaries continue to base their expositions on treatises by European authors and no-one ventures to study the special forms which actually exist in local legal practise.

Also, civil regulations are canonised, such as the procedure for the inscription and rectification of parochial records, taken from the Code of Civil Procedures by the Eighth Provincial Council of Lima in 1928, because of the needs of the local situation.

This being the case, it can be seen that the problem is rooted in the difficulty of adapting canonical structures to Andean reality. The plan for a diocesan curia prepared by the Pontifical Commission 'de recognoscendo C.I.C.' would be nothing short of utopian for the Andean dioceses, and special concessions will have to be made. This is what happened at the end of the plenary Council in 1899, when Pope Leo XIII had to make special concessions which were to be valid for thirty years but were renewed up to Vatican II.

1. MATTERS TO BE DISCUSSED WITH THE ROMAN CURIA

Since Vatican II, the matters needing to be discussed with the Roman curia have decreased notably. In former years bishops enjoyed quinquennial (in the case of Latin America decennial) faculties which relieved them of the necessity of referring a number of matters to Rome. Some of these matters could be settled by Apostolic Nuncios, thanks to the powers delegated to them by the Holy See.

The Episcopal Conference makes representations which are of such a nature as to apply generally to the whole country. In some cases the Roman curia used to require each bishop to apply directly to Rome, but the Conference drew attention to the useless multiplication of identical applications. In other cases the opinion of the Conference is asked on a diocesan or regional application, with the frequent result that it is dealt with by the Conference itself.

In fact communications from each bishopric to the Holy See are very few, and I personally have not had much correspondence with the Roman curia.

2. COMMUNICATION WITH THE ROMAN CURIA

Frequently communications from the Roman curia are sent to the Episcopal Conference (formerly to the nunciature), and the president of the Conference replies in the name of the episcopate. Direct communications are relatively rare and are limited to the sending of general directions.

My experience of dealing with the Roman curia over a period of thirty years in the Archdiocese of Lima, first as a member of the diocesan curia and then for the last sixteen years in Cajamarca, indicates that petitions should be definite and precise.

It is helpful that the Roman curia includes, along with older Europeans who know Latin America, a number of officials born in the continent who are better informed on the situation. However, account must be taken of the fact that actual conditions in a metropolis like Buenos Aires are very different from the Andean situation, and a knowledge of the Colombian plateau of Cundinamarca does not imply familiarity with the problems of the high plateau of Collao in the Andes of Peru and Bolivia. Moreover a young continent changes rapidly in many respects, and in the space of a few years the experts can easily find themselves out of touch. The same thing happens with the officials of the various Aid Agencies (Adveniat, Misereor, Cebemo, Latin American Bureau, etc.).

It is for this reason that very frequently the responses of the Roman curia are of a very general nature and do not contribute much to the solution of problems. Similarly, forms of enquiry are devised for situations other than our own, and it is difficult to answer the questions accurately. There is a real danger of sticking to the letter 'to please the nuncio', as someone put it, and so distorting the facts.

A few years ago the attention of the Central Office of Statistics of the Secretariat of State was drawn to the enormous disproportion between the number of baptisms administered and the number of marriages celebrated. In reply I submitted a paper showing how in practice it was not common to receive the sacramental blessing for a widely observed pre-Colombian custom.

3. QUINQUENNIAL RELATIONS; VISITS *AD LIMINA*

The forms for the quinquennial enquiries have also changed in recent years: that is to say, they have been simplified. But because they are sent out to the whole Church it is not easy to show the true situation. A few decades ago a nuncio said, referring to the forms and the answers received: 'The bishops do not lie, but they do not tell the truth.' In the same way the observations of the Roman curia are equally generalised, and make no contribution to the solution of the problems.

We bishops of Latin America should make the visit 'ad limina' every ten years. The diocese of Cajamarca has existed for almost seventy years, and during that time no bishop has made the visit, by reason of the world wars, or infirmity, or the vacancy of the see. A visit is planned for 1979, with the help of God.

On the occasion of the Council and other visits to Rome I have approached the Vatican departments on some issues of national importance, but hardly ever on diocesan affairs.

4. THE LANGUAGE BARRIER: STYLE OF THE ROMAN DOCUMENTS

For the last twenty years or so there has been no difficulty over addressing the Roman curia in Spanish, and often the replies come in the same language. There is therefore no linguistic problem whatever.

However, the style of the documents is still very curialistic, in contrast with the simple way in which recent popes have expressed themselves. It seems to me that it is a difficulty of an academic and clerical kind, resulting from the education we have received. Being a university man, and moreover one brought up in the capital, I myself find it impossible to write in a style suitable for the Andean peasants. These are human limitations, and they call for a profound conversion. It is different when I speak with the peasants, because in dialogue one rapidly becomes aware of not being understood and one makes an effort to find an appropriate expression or illustration.

Because of the great number and the urgency of pastoral duties at diocesan and national level it is impossible to subject the actual situation to scrutiny in the light of canonical principles in order to try to interpret it; and at the same time the professors of canon law confine themselves to explaining the Code academically along the lines laid down by European canonists without going more deeply into practical questions, and they lack the creativity which might enable them to discover new forms of expression. They might say, in answer to an enquiry, that something 'is not in conformity with the law', but they do not realise that the law has to come to terms with reality.

The reason why we often live outside the legal limits is that it is largely forgotten that justice is wider than the formal law.

Translated by G. W. S. Knowles

Jan Heijke

Communication between the African Church and the Roman Curia

THE SECOND Vatican Council stressed the importance of 'local' churches and, with a clear desire to promote decentralisation, placed greater emphasis on the office of the bishop in the Church. At the same time, it also called for the reorganisation of the Roman curia, for a clearer distinction to be made between the function of the papal legates and the responsibilities of the local bishops and for the latter to be given a more active part to play in the central government of the Church.[1]

We now know how these demands were satisfied. The curia was re-organised in such a way that authority was concentrated in the person of the papal secretary of state. There was also a positive reaction to the call for greater participation on the part of diocesan bishops. In the case of the Congregation for the Evangelisation of the Peoples, for example, it was decided to allow certain diocesan bishops, appointed by the pope, to attend some of the plenary sessions of this department, with the right to vote if the pope saw fit.[2]

Finally, the function of the papal legates was redefined. A mellifluous sentence such as 'through his envoys, the pope participates in the life of his sons and their needs and most intimate desires can be more easily made known to him through them'[3] cannot disguise the fact that a deliberate policy of centralisation was being carried out. The legates were given a stronger position with regard to the bishops and the bishops' conferences were kept at a distance from the central government of the Church. The papal nuncio rather than the conference of bishops was the intermediary between the local church and Rome. It was in this and similar ways that the recommendations of Vatican II were carried out.

1. ROMAN CENTRALISATION IN AFRICA

It is well known that the African provinces of the Church are still connected to the Congregation for the Evangelisation of the Peoples as closely as if they were tied by an umbilical cord. They are seen institutionally as churches that are young, still growing and in need of help. It would, of course, be a great distinction for all Christian churches if they thought of themselves as being in a learning position with regard to Jesus and the gospel, but this separate provision for the 'young' churches points to a difference in status. It suggests, in other words, that they have not yet come of age and are still dependent. There have been many indications, for example, in interventions made during synods, that the African bishops do not like their churches to be regarded as branches of white missionary churches. The African contribution to the Congregation for the Evangelisation of the Peoples is, moreover, quite considerable. Five of the thirty-nine cardinals and two of the fifteen bishops who are members of this department of the Roman curia reside in Africa. Of the forty-five consultors, three are African diocesan bishops.[4]

Since the demand was made in 1965 at the Second Vatican Council that the function of the papal nuncios should be more precisely defined, more and more Vatican representatives have been sent to Africa. When the Decree *Christus Dominus* on the Bishops' Office in the Church was promulgated in 1965, there were ten nuncios in Africa. Now there are forty-two.[4] In most of the African provinces of the Church, then, the papal nuncio is a post-conciliar phenomenon, but his powers are pre-conciliar.

In another way too, the papal nuncio is a newcomer to the continent. Thirty-one of the forty-two nuncios are Italians and the rest include a Yugoslav, an Irishman, a Belgian, a German, an American and a Frenchman.[5] To judge by the course of events in Africa, it would seem that Rome has tried above all to avoid the possibility of an identification between its representatives and the local community of believers. All the nuncios are from the West and none of them stay very long. They were all trained at the Pontificia Accademia Ecclesiastica in Rome and they change their post frequently. They are required to serve anywhere in the world,[6] to remain outsiders and to have a deep knowledge of and commitment to curial diplomacy.

Yet, according to the *Motu Proprio* of 1969, their most important task is not contact with the government of the country in which they are serving, but the promotion of unity between the local churches and the

Apostolic See. Their commitment should be to spiritual well-being (*bonum animarum*).[7] It is almost a commonplace to say that African culture differs from North Atlantic culture, but, if initiatives taken by the African Christian community have to be judged by the papal nuncios— and they do that *coram Deo,* which means without any checks being kept on them and under cover of secrecy—then familiarity with the situation in Africa ought to be a pre-requisite for the post. Now, however, because of the status of papal representation in Africa and the way in which the posts have in fact been filled, there is almost no opportunity for the voice of Africa to be effectively heard in Rome.

In principle, of course, it would be possible for African bishops to withdraw young African priests from pastoral work in their own countries and send them to Rome to be trained in papal diplomacy. In fact, however, the bishops prefer to let the few priests whom they have at their disposal train in ways that are more directly related to the pastoral concerns of their churches.

2. THE REACTION OF THE AFRICAN EPISCOPATE

Whatever disappointments they may have experienced at the hands of the curia, many of the African bishops seem, perhaps for the sake of safety, to assume that it is preferable not to try to judge the interaction between themselves and the Holy See, at least in public. The Roman authorities themselves have been at pains to preserve the impression that even the idea of an assessment is disrespectful.[8] The central offices of the Church should be obeyed, not subjected to criticism. Whenever the African bishops make their concerns in this question of interaction known to Rome, they often wrap them up in such extravagant expressions of loyalty to the Holy Father that any corrective influence that these interventions might have on the way in which the Church functions at the top is seriously weakened in advance.

Since 1969, the African bishops have been organised on a continental scale in the Symposium of the Episcopal Conferences of Africa and Madagascar (S.E.C.A.M.). Even at the first meeting of S.E.C.A.M. in 1969, resolutions were passed that the cover of curial secrecy should be removed and the term *sub secreto* on Roman documents should be replaced by another formula, such as 'not intended for publication'. It was even suggested that the decision as to whether texts were to be secret or not should be made not by the curia, but by the episcopates concerned. A demystification of this kind would have made it possible to study curial interventions and responses in a circle that was wider than that of the African bishops. Everything, however, points to the great reluctance, at least for the present, of the curia to abandon this element of power that is so essential to its function—and that of the nuncios.

Indeed, every attempt is made by the curia to limit the harm that can be done by inevitable publicity. One example of this is the intervention at the bishops' conference in Rome in 1974. Bishop Sangu of Tanzania was to have provided a panoramic view of the Church in Africa in the name of the bishops of the whole continent. This survey contained a section on the nunciature: 'Following the signs of our times and the thinking of most countries of Africa, we humbly ask the Holy See to see to it that the image of the Vatican Diplomatic Corps take a moral universal (Catholic) character than the present one, which is seen as "mostly Italian". It is painful to hear now and then accusations that the Vatican (the Holy See) is practising nationalism in the Catholic Church. We also feel that it is necessary to revise the terms of competence of the Vatican Diplomatic Corps in relationship to the local churches (Episcopal Conferences) and to the local governments in Africa. Since the establishment of the Episcopal Conferences, it is good (and necessary) to clarify the boundaries of duties and competence of the Episcopal Conference and those of the Vatican Diplomatic Corps in relation to ecclesiastical matters of the local church and in relation to the Vatican and the Sacred Congregation'.

The urgent need to clarify the boundaries of competence was taken seriously by the curia, which responded with alacrity by taking care of the English text of the African bishops' statement and making a Latin version of it. It was this Latin text that was beautifully printed and distributed among the assembled bishops. It is interesting to note the difference between the original passage quoted above and this passage in the new Latin text which corresponds to it: 'The legates sent by the Supreme Pontiff to the nations of the world show forth the universal character of the Church and display the care that the Church has for all the needs of mankind while carrying out the work of evangelisation. The better these legates who are drafted to the public authority of the nations can combine their work with that of the Episcopal Conferences and the local churches of Africa, the more this will promote the work of the whole Church in the need to evangelise this immense continent'.[9]

Despite the words of warning uttered by Pope Paul VI at the end of the 1974 Synod, the African bishops again expressed their wishes with regard to the curia and nunciatures a year later at their S.E.C.A.M. conference. They also called for changes in the law in certain important areas in canon law, such as marriage and the office of the priesthood.

We can, of course, say more about the wishes expressed by the representatives of the African Church than about the *desiderata* to which Rome has conceded. One thing, however, is certain—the repeated requests for recognition of the African Church's different character have not been made because of prejudice against the Holy See. They have arisen because of disappointments and humiliating experiences caused by the central governing body of the Church and because of the African bishops' sense of pastoral responsibility for those entrusted to their care.

The complaints are above all concerned with the structure. The good intentions of individual nuncios are not necessarily called into question. Some keep themselves very much in the background. Others regard themselves as real detectors and send brain-storming papers to Rome. They believe that the prompt registration of a deviation from the norm will prevent disaster.

A few examples will show what I mean by this. One papal legate in East Africa sent a letter to the episcopate there outling in detail his objections to a recipe for baking hosts.[10] Another legate made it known that he believed that the teaching content in the syllabus offered to candidates for the priesthood in a very poor little training college was insufficient. Another nuncio called on the local bishop to change the minutes of a meeting of the deanery of priests, in such a way that the report of the deliberations would be in accordance with the views of the nuncio himself, as the only one whose opinions were acceptable. Although they have no experience of pastoral work and no knowledge of the country in which they are serving, these diplomats set themselves up as pastors and even as supreme pastors in a part of the world with a totally different culture from their own. Sometimes, fortunately, a nuncio takes the trouble to learn the language of the people and to help out in a parish on Sundays. There are, however, very few cases known to us of nuncios taking up the cause of church communities with bold, resourceful plans. Most of the evidence gathered at random in Africa points to indifference, disappointment or annoyance.

3. PEOPLE ARE INVOLVED

The flow of information in pastoral matters in Africa has to pass through the bottleneck of the nunciatures and be analysed and tested before it is allowed to reach the customers who need it. This causes great delays and even stagnation. Far from regretting this, the curia seems almost to intend to slow the process down. We will confine ourselves here to two examples which illustrate this slowness to the point of stagnation in matters of urgent pastoral care in Africa—marriage and the priesthood.

There has been for very many years an impressive measure of agreement among pastoral workers in Africa about the unsuitability of the Church's law on marriage with regard to Africa. For eleven centuries in Europe, the practice of *mariage coutumier,* as it has come to be known, was normal. In this form, marriage was contracted in accordance with the custom of the extended family and without the necessary intervention of the Church—the presence at the ceremony of a priest was optional—but regarded as valid and accepted by the Church. In an attempt to safeguard marriage as an institution subject to public law, the Council of Trent prescribed, on pain of invalidity, that a qualified witness—in this case, a priest—should be present at the marriage contract. Marriage was in this way made a Church matter and the earlier practice of secular marriage was declared invalid.

There are not many priests working in Africa who are familiar with the history of marriage in the Church, but they have done their best to introduce this model of marriage. They have, however, fond that most baptised African Catholics are regarded officially as incomplete Christians and even as public sinners, exluded from the sacraments.[11] This is because of the application of the canonical laws of marriage without reference to the different cultural situation in Africa.

The public character of the marriage contract has always been recognised in Africa, but, despite all the efforts made by the African bishops to convince the Roman authorities that the canon laws regarding marriage cannot be observed on the continent, they have been told again and again that their plea cannot be admitted or that they should study the whole question at a deeper level. Sometimes the curia even goes so far as to intervene to prevent action from being taken. 'That kind of person can only be convinced by prayer and fasting', the president of one African bishops' conference wrote once in the diocesan bulletin, after having recorded another rejection from Rome.

Let us now briefly consider our second example. The curia has on several occasions intervened to prevent the Church's offices from being adapted to the situation in Africa. Every year, many Africans are admitted to baptism. In this way, the Church accepts the obligation to help these neophytes towards faith and to administer the sacraments to them. This, however, is a promise that cannot be kept. As we have seen, however, the curia has obliged the African bishops to impose a strict censorship on themselves and this has proved to be so effective that very few bishops have ventured to ask Rome for permission to ordain suitable married men to preside at the Eucharist. They put a good face on it and explain to people in the villages that they can be fed just as well by the Word of God throughout the many months that will pass until the odd foreign priest comes and for a little while makes their little Christian community into a real church.

It is, of course, possible to be cheerful and to avoid the extremes of bitterness and irony. But it is not possible to avoid the impression that the curia is trying to eliminate all opposition and to reduce the pastoral responsibility of the African episcopate to pure obedience. There was a period in the Church's history when patriarchates or 'rites' were able to emerge. The African Church was born too late for this. It is, however, worth noting a letter written in 1534 by the papal nuncio in Lisbon to the Secretary of State in Rome, Carnesecchi, shortly after Pope Leo X had given the Maronites permission to have their own church: 'In my opinion, it is necessary to give the priests (of the Congo) permission to marry, as has been done for the Maronites'.[12]

The ordination of married men is only one example of a much deeper problem. It is really a question of whether the Church is to be truly universal or whether the North Atlantic Church is to continue to impose its own tradition and hegemony on a subject and dependent African Church. It is only if the Church in Africa is allowed to be itself that it will be able to contribute to the catholicity of the whole Church.

Translated by David Smith

Notes

1. Decree *Christus Dominus* on the Bishops' Office in the Church, 1965, 9 and 10.

2. *Acta Apostolicae Sedis* 59 (1967), 916, No. 83.

3. Motu Proprio: *Sollicitudo omnium ecclesiarum, Acta Apostolicae Sedis* 61 (1969) pp. 475-476.

4. *Annuario Pontificio* (1977).

5. op. cit. Sometimes one person is entrusted with more than one legation. This is certainly the case in Africa, with the result that the ratio is fifteen Italians to six others, all of North Atlantic origin.

6. The nuncio serving in Central Africa was appointed papal legate to Cuba in 1976. He was replaced by another Italian who had served in Costa Rica, Chile, the Philippines, Yugoslavia and Korea. This career is not at all unusual.

7. *Acta Apostolicae Sedis* 61 (1969), 480. V. 1.

8. The formula *Personam Sanctae Sedis* was inserted—rather generously—into the job description of papal legates by the curia. This gives an (illusory) impression that the prerogatives of the Petrine office can be multiplied at will.

9. The Latin text of this passage is as follows: Ipsae Legationes quas Summus Pontifex mittit ad nationes mundi ostendunt indolem universalem Ecclesiae atque comprobant curam quam Ecclesia gerit de omnibus necessitatibus hominum, dum opus evangelizationis prosequitur. Quo melius hi Legati apud publicas nationum auctoritates constituti suam operam coniunxerint cum Conferentiis Episcopalibus et Ecclesiis localibus Africae, eo magis expedietur opus totius Ecclesiae in evangelizanda immensa illa Continenti.

10. See the *African Ecclesiastical Review* 17 (1975) p. 120 and 18 (1976) pp. 213-217.

11. See *Pro Mundi Vita,* Dossier Africain 2 (1976) p. 49 and Michel Legrain's excellent book: *Mariage Chrétien, Modèle Unique? Questions Venues d'Afrique* (Paris 1978).

12. L. Jadin *Correspondance de Dom Affonso, Roi du Congo, 1506-1543,* (Brussels 1974) p. 195. In an intervention in the Synod held in Rome in 1971, Mgr. J. N'Dayen, the Archbishop of Bangui, Central Africa, pointed out that it was purely accidental and fortuitous that his part of Africa belonged to the Latin rite.

Part III

Projecting Collegial Institutions into the Future

René Laurentin

Synod and Curia

ON SEPTEMBER 15 1965, as the last session of the Second Vatican Council opened, Paul VI finalised the foundation of the Synod of Bishops. It was the principal institution created in the upshot of the Council.

Since that time the Synod has held five sessions, from 1967 to 1977. It has aroused great hopes and has produced equally great disillusion. Commentators had envisaged it, perhaps prematurely, as the organ of a collegial re-structuring in Roman government. In fact it has exercised no power, and taken neither initiative nor decision.[1]

Why was this institution founded? Why has it remained ineffective and marginal? Why has it burdened with fresh obligations that very papal government whose reduction it was the Synod's own task to achieve? Why have the fathers at the different Synods shown themselves to be enthusiasts, despite all this, for their inconsequential reunions? What can one expect for the future, since John Paul II, from his inaugural discourse onwards, has expressed his intention to promote the Synod? And what impact will this itself have on the re-structuring of the curia—the object of this issue of *Concilium*?

To reply adequately to these questions we must reconsider:

1. The origins of the Synod;
2. Its ambiguous experimental condition under Paul VI;
3. Its future.

1. THE ORIGINS OF THE SYNOD

The constitution of the Church

The coming into existence of the Synod in the first place corresponds to an essential feature of the Church's own constitution. According to

Christ's founding ordinance her apostolic government is essentially collegiate. If the Church is to be what he has willed, this collegiality has to
find organs and forms of expression. These forms may be, and are, of the
most diverse kinds, according to the particularities of tradition in the
Christian east or the Christian west, and depending on period and culture.

Historical expression

At Rome itself in the medieval period the pope governed with the
assistance of the *Concilium Romanum,* or Roman Synod,[2] a gathering of
those bishops who were resident within two hundred kilometres of the
See of Peter. The distance amounted to two days' journey, a gauge which
today would include the whole world. These bishops of suburbican dioceses, i.e., dioceses bordering on that of Rome, made up the central core
of what was, therefore, a kind of permanent Synod.

When in the twelfth century the election of the pope was reserved to
the cardinals the latter became the foremost individuals in the Church[3]
and before long the exclusive counsellors of the pope. The cardinalatial
council, operating under the name of 'consistory', increasingly internationalised in practice but dignified by the fiction that every cardinal was
a titular Roman parish priest, came to supplant the Synod. After the
conciliarist crisis the popes reduced the consistories to the simplest possible elements. During these last centuries the cardinals no longer spoke.
Rather, they listened to the pope. Their sole activity in council was to
offer a gesture of tacit and unconditional approval. In fact, by the end of
the pontificate of Pius XII the collegial dimension of the Church had been
reduced to that simplest expression which consists in having a few organs
of witness. The theologians of the Roman court, indeed, were beginning
to say that councils of any kind, useful though they may have been in the
days when papal infallibility and primacy were not fully defined, had now
become superflous. The First Vatican Council, it was alleged, had
brought the era of councils to a close by recognising the plenary powers of
the pope. The future lay solely with the development of absolute monarchy. Collegiality could no longer be more than a docile and subordinate
instrument, a way of experiencing papal communion and obedience. The
very word became suspect and was on the way to excision from the official
vocabulary. This distrust continued for several years after the Council.

The experience of Vatican II

The Synod was born from an experience of what the Church is. This
was the experience of the Council convoked by John XXIII and first and
foremost of that Council's Preparatory Central Commission, presided

over by the pope himself. This assembly, one hundred strong, included many of the principal office-bearers of the Church: fifty-nine cardinals (more than two-thirds of the College), five patriarchs, thirty-one bishops and five religious. The Commission proved to be a parliament, in the original sense of that word—a place to speak. Projects for reform were aired there by Cardinals Liénart, Frings, Montini, Koenig, Doepfner, Alfrink, Bea and, last but not least, by the patriarch Maximos IV. (This list is given in the order then customary.) As early as November 1961 Cardinal Alfrink had expressed in public at Nijmegen his hope that such a group might come into effective existence as one of the Church's governmental organs.

The utopia of Maximos IV

It was in this body, then, that the discussion of collegiality was re-opened. It found its strongest and most audacious, indeed utopian, expression in the speech of Maximos IV at the last session of the Council, on November 6 1963, at midday:

> The concrete task of assisting the pope in the general governance of the Church . . . must revert to a limited group of bishops, drawn from the entire world and representing the college. This group could form the true Sacred College of the universal Church. It would comprise the principal bishops in the Church. In the first place they would be the patriarchs resident in apostolic sees, such as the Oecumenical Councils of the first centuries recognised; next would come cardinal archbishops, but under the titles of their cathedrals, not of Roman parishes; lastly there would be bishops chosen by the episcopal conference of each country. . . .
>
> But naturally, that in itself would not suffice. There must be in constant session at Rome what the eastern Church calls a *synodos endimousa,* i.e., a number of members of this apostolic and universal Sacred College succeeding each other by turns at the pope's side as . . . the supreme . . . executive and decision-making council of the worldwide Church. All the Roman departments must be subject to this. (Original French text in R. Laurentin *Bilan de la deuxième session* (Paris 1964) p. 118.)

Amid the day-to-day activity of the Council, something which has left little trace in historical record, a Chilean *peritus* accompanying Cardinal Silva Enriquez worked efficently but discreetly to gain signatories for a petition to the pope asking for the restoration of a Synod. It obtained about five hundred signatures, five times more than a petition circulated by the same *peritus* for reform of the Holy Office. This last picked up no more than a hundred or so signatures, for fear of penalisation.

Paul VI's initiatives and decisions

Maximos IV's petition and speech had been made possible by some discreetly worded overtures contained in the discourses of Paul VI. These date from a speech of September 29 1963: 'The Council must reinforce . . . the means (*rationes*) at our disposal in exercising our apostolic function. . . . This universal function, although endowed by Christ, as you are aware, with a fulness of power and a legitimate authority to empower action, could nevertheless be augmented by a greater effectiveness. . . . If only brother bishops could lend us a more considerable and informed active assistance in the charge we have received—by whatever meausres and means might appropriately be invoked.'[4] The Council fathers replied to this initiative of the pope in their own interventions and petitions. So it was that Paul VI came to found the Synod on September 15 1965.

2. THE AMBIGUITY OF THE SYNOD

A supreme collegial assembly

According to its own founding decree, the Synod is an organ whose purpose lies in 'the perpetuation of the benefits of the Council, by assisting the pope in his charge as universal pastor'. It is an expression of collegial communion with an ordinary 'mission' of 'information and counsel'. But Paul VI also envisaged that it might have 'a power of decision-making . . . at such a time as that is bestowed (*collata*) upon the Synod by the Sovereign Pontiff'.

The Synod has a character described as being 'perpetual of its very nature'. By this formula the pope was giving a guarantee against any attempted suppression of what is a constitutional organ.

It is representative: the Synod is composed of elected representatives to the tune of eighty per cent (as compared with sixty per cent for the cardinalatial commissions). The remaining percentage derives from members nominated by the pope (fifteen per cent) and the heads of curial departments.

The pope is personally the president of the Synod, and this at a time (since 1967) when he no longer presides over any of the Roman congregations, not even over the Holy Office which formerly held itself to be the 'supreme congregation' precisely because of such papal presidency.[5]

All of this provides the basis for Edward Schillebeeckx' comment that the Synod's activity is 'in the strictest sense a collegial, though not a conciliar, affair'.[6]

The narrow limits of the Synod

Why is it, then, that this supreme organ has remained honorific and impotent, even to the point of being considered as irremediably so by some theologians of collegiality? The reason lies in the conditions of its creation, which were restrictive, irresponsible and subordinationist:

1.The pope has not established this institution through the agency of the Council. He has in a real sense granted it existence by a purely personal act, in the typical form of the *Motu Proprio.* It appears, therefore, to be an adjunct to the primacy rather than an expression of collegiality.

2. The Synod has been brought into existence, at each moment and in every relationship constitutive of that existence, in the most complete imaginable dependence on the pope. It is he alone who convokes the Synod, who fixes its venue and who ratifies the election of its members. (They become such only on his nomination.) The pope and the pope alone determines the agenda (Article 1 of its regulating document)[7] and names not only the secretaries (Articles 12 and 13) and the chairmen of committees (Article 28) but also the overall president or presidents who themselves take the chair in the name of the pope himself (Article 3). The decision to authorise a vote in the Synod is reserved to the pope (Article 22); most important, it is he who determines whether such a vote is to be merely consultative or genuinely deliberative, i.e., fully executive. Finally, even in this last hypothetical case—for the contingency has never been realised so far—it has been made perfectly clear that it pertains 'to the Sovereign Pontiff and to him alone to decide upon the votes taken'. In other words, it is for the pope to ratify or to reject the decisions that the Synod might vote.

3. Although according to its founding charter the Synod is supposed to be 'perpetual' it is in fact intermittent. Basically the Synod has no existence outside of its sessions unless this be in the form of its Secretariat. Now the permanent secretary of the Synod is a curial functionary named by the pope and not by the Synod itself. He has never figured in the list of persons with a right to regular audience, but it is the frequency of such audience which is the measure of power at Rome. The notorious *Tabella* is no longer printed but practice still conforms closely with it. Furthermore, the secretariat of the Synod is linked administratively with the pope not directly but through the mediation of the Council for the Public Business of the Church which is a kind of ecclesiastical Foreign Office.

4. The length of the intervals at which the Synod meets is also a factor. The most responsibly behaved Synod, that of 1969, settled for two-year intervals but this has now been spaced out to every third year.

5. The Synod had frequently exercised its powers in a subservient

spirit. With the exception of the 1969 Synod it has accepted as kind of internal tacit law that nothing should be done, or even proposed, without some prior assurance that it is in all respects in accordance with the pope's wishes. Whoever has departed from this unformulated norm has paid the price.[8]

6. During the Synods, and especially since 1971, people have repeated ad nauseam the slogans that 'the Synod is not a Council (*un Concile*). It is only for counsel (*un conseil*)'. The press was conditioned by official sources to orchestrate these slogans, sometimes quite obsessively. People add that the Synod is without power. It is not appropriate, they say, that the Synod should exercise power and the pope has done it a signal service in refusing to grant it a deliberating voice. The Synod is a locus of affective, not effective, collegiality. Its strength and value lie in the collegial communion which grows by means of it and not in any pseudo-problems about powers.

This unbelievable accumulation of restrictions is truly astonishing. It relates to the ancient fear that has reduced to merely witnessing status any organs of a democratic type which might limit papal power. This is an historic heritage of the Holy See stemming from its patient struggle to win power over the secular rulers who threatened the Church—and from a consistent resolve to impose its will in whatever circumstance. A power is all the stronger when there is no other opposed to it. These restrictions may also be traced to the personal temperament of Paul VI, given to disquiet as he was at all that might interfere with papal power and papal psychology. It was a fear all the more potent in that he knew himself to be so easily disarmed, as much by his goodness as by his timidity, before an interlocutor in a face-to-face encounter. In such a way he barricaded his power. He would not accept dialogue with others of divergent views unless he were first assured of their agreement on whatever fundamentals were at stake in the meeting.

An apparent contradiction

So there is an apparent contradiction between the fundamental structure of the Synod and the restrictive framework of its procedural rules and its functioning in day-to-day practice. Collegiality is here shackled.

These shackles may be explained to a considerable degree by the experimental character of the Synod, by a concern that awareness of collegiality should come about in a gradual way without precipitating irreversible situations.

Hypotheses for the future

All that has been said so far should not deprive Paul VI of praise which is rightfully his. The Synod he established in a germinal form is fundamentally well-constituted and soundly structured as a body called to be a supreme organ of the Church. Futhermore, Paul VI was sufficiently encouraged by the harmonious and docile way the Synod set about its business to free it from certain impediments and limits. For instance in 1969 he set up a council of twelve bishops whose task was to ensure continuity between Synods.

The artificial restrictions and limits under which the Synod labours could be lifted tomorrow if only the pope would give the Synod a remit of initiative and responsibility befitting its high vocation.

It is not a question of developing a democratic institution out of the Synod. If the election of eighty per cent of the members of the Synod may be referred to as a democratic process—one which, it may be noted, surpasses the demands of Maximos IV—that is not what the Church is about. Her law is not the majority game but the play of communion and unanimity in which the Holy Spirit sets the rules. Neither is it a question of reverting to the superiority of the college of bishops over the pope in that line of descent from the Council of Constance which saved the Church by deposing three popes. There is no intention of contesting the superiority of the pope over the college, a superiority reconquered in an extreme version by the papacy in the centuries that followed Constance. Rather what is wanted is some effort to transcend the relations of superiority and inferiority, some attempt to recognise the organic character of the college, a college that includes essentially and constitutively the primacy of the pope. In the end this amounts to saying that we should recognise one single subject of power in the Church, a subject which may act in two ways, with endless possibilities of modulation between them. Power in the Church may be exercised monarchically or collegially, the pope remaining always judge and master of the situation in the last resort.

Within this monarchical college (or within this collegial monarchy, if the phrase be preferred), the Synod's vocation is to promote not only communion, dialogue and practical exchange but a co-responsibility in which through common effort, and therefore participation in and sharing of obligations, the bishops may 'unburden' the pope (to use the phrase allowed during the Council) of duties, rather than adding to them a supplementary set (convoking the Synod, following its course, turning into formulae a mass of informal interventions) without subtracting any—the situation which has pertained until now.

This is in fact the aim expressed by John Paul II right from his inaugural discourse of October 1978. He proposes to 'promote' and 'deepen collegiality', the very essence of Church government, and to 'develop to this end organs that are partly new, partly refurbished, above all the Synod of Bishops'.

Beyond the tensions between Conciliarism and pontifical absolutism we are urged on to restore in a balanced form the primordial governance of the Church as founded by Christ: that collegiality which implies a primacy, that primacy which takes its own measure in terms of charity within the community of the college, charity both affective and effective.

3. SYNOD AND CURIA

When all these implications are explored it is a simple task to see the fresh light the Synod has brought to relations between the curia and the two poles of supreme government—the pope and the bishops. We may look at this in three of its aspects:

Internationalisation of the curia

In Counter-Reformation ecclesiology (Palmieri etc.), the curia was presented as the organ and instrument of the pope. Thanks to its permanence and to the privilege of irremovability which the curia had negotiated with each pope over the course of centuries, it exercised absolutism in the mode of its reign over the bishops and frequently enough secrecy in the style of its proceedings. The least curial prelate, even when not a bishop, might say, as people used to say in the pre-Conciliar curia, 'When I carry out my function, I am the pope'.

The Council has knocked all false mystique out of this situation. Both its aura and its abuses have been transformed by the restoration of effective, smooth and equitable communication between curia and bishops. The Synod has proved a meeting-point of equals in the deliberations that have gone on there between the heads of congregational tribunals, those who are Synod members by right and the bishops elected by majority vote who represent the churches of the whole world.

This equal footing is all the better established in that the internationalisation of the curia, whereby diocesan bishops are now candidates for the most important posts (Secretary of State, Prefects of the Congregation for the Doctrine of the Faith, the Congregation for the Evangelisation of Peoples, the Congregation for the Clergy, the Congregation for Catholic Education and so forth), has itself brought to an end the 'barrier' and 'difference of level'[9] which made membership of the curia a career for a closed group, recruited from within a charmed circle by co-option, the whole system being reinforced whenever the pope was elected from within the curia—as every attempt was made so to elect him.

The humiliation of the curia

The loss of the privilege of irremovability and Paul VI's draconian personal reformation of the curia from 1967 onwards have tended to produce similar consequences. The pope has obliged the curia to submit at all points. He has made it strictly subordinate to the offices of the

Secretariat of State which now control and shadow practically every curial department and put their own finishing touches to all curial projects, normally without offering consultation and in top secret. The curia is inhibited and humbled, virtually to the point where its normal functioning is suffering.[10]

Repercussions for papal Conclaves

Diocesan bishops and bishops working with the pope in Rome itself have thus become interchangeable and in solidarity with each other. They feel themselves to be today on a level footing of collegial brotherhood. The web of common responsibilities provides a tissue of collegial relationships that have proved of great benefit in the two conclaves of 1978 where the excellent personal relations formed at Synods provided the materials of responsible papal electioneering. A choice of pope at once became possible from among candidates outside the restricted circle of the curia and of Italy.

The conclaves have enhanced the position of the Sacred College, enfeebled by the Synod, in so far as the distinction between simple bishop and cardinal (so striking at the Council) had become whittled down and relativised. Paul VI briefly entertained a plan to level off this distinction still further by giving the permanent council of the Synod (and the patriarchs) access to the conclave. He renounced this plan in the face of multifarious objections of which one at least was serious and well-founded. To elect the pope no longer on the basis, however fictitious, that the cardinals are the representatives of the Roman people but on the basis of a gathering representative of the Church universal, would be gravely to undermine a principle fundamental to tradition, namely that the pope is only pope as bishop of Rome. He is pope because he is bishop of a local church not some sort of super-bishop of the kind dreamt of by dangerous technocratically minded men for whom the Holy See of Rome is only a stepping-stone. A super-episcopal pope who would no longer be the Roman bishop or who would only be the Roman bishop by an increasingly tenuous fiction would be a scandal for the eastern tradition, founded as that tradition is on the existence and collegiality of local church communities. That tradition protects us from the abuses to which the Latin conception of the Church, juridicist and polarised on the matter of power, is only too tempted.

The electoral principle

To this may be added a factor of a different kind which does not submit easily to evaluation. I refer to the restoration of the electoral principle in the constitution of the Synod and of its permanent council. This has brought particular bishops into the limelight by means of election, world-wide in scope and decentralised in implication, rather than by way of the personal (or curial) will of the pope. This cannot be without effect in the future. To give one example: before nominating a prefect for the Holy Office who would be neither a man of the Holy Office nor a man of the curia the pope waited until the election of a commission at the Synod had pushed Cardinal Seper to the forefront. He made him prefect of the Holy Office with the support of Synodal votes.[11]

The supreme organ of collegiality

In what concerns the relations between curia and Synod the crucial problem for the future is this: by reforming the Synod (August 6 1967) Paul VI created two collegial institutions of the top rank:

> 1. The Synod, at the level of the Church universal;
> 2. The council of heads of curial offices, chief focus of communication and collegial co-responsibility in the curia. This council is constructed on the traditional plan of the 'congregation' which has given its name to the great departments of the Roman curia.[12] It is convoked and presided over by the secretary of state who in this respect has a role comparable to that of a Prime Minister or President of a Council of Ministers.

As with the Synod, this second collegial institution has not been allowed to take top-level decisions. No more than the Synod is it the real locus of power. Indeed, the pope has taken the chair at its meetings only on the most exceptional occasions, in sharp contrast with the Synod where he has been personally present throughout.

How will the relation between the Synod, its permanent council and the council of heads of curial bureaux come to be expressed? To what extent will the pope come to be the personal president of these last two institutions? This is a key question, for where the pope is, there is power.

If the Synod of Bishops is freed from restriction and permitted to function normally, according to its proper role in the Church, it is the Synod that will become in normal conditions the supreme organ of government. It will gather within its embrace both the bishops and the departmental heads of the curia. Its permanent council, once again presided over normally by the pope, would become the place where major decisions are taken and the means by which they are carried out: what Maximos IV called a *synodos endimousa*. This framework would provide for a sharing of responsibilities with the pope and hence for relieving him of some of his burdens, burdens which, in the sense of personal decision-making, multiplied under Paul VI. If such a promotion of the Synod came about, along the path outlined by John Paul II, the secretary of the Synod would become the first public servant of the Church. For, despite all changes of title and title-bearer over the course of generations, the Church's first servant is always the man who sees the pope most. On this hypothesis of participatory government with a division of collegial labour, the secretary of the Synod would be the man whose contacts would be most frequent with both the pope and those associated with him in the work of government.

If such a promotion of the Synod were brought about, the pope would find himself obliged eventually to select between two hypotheses that have some support in the present situation. Either the secretary of the Synod will become the right-hand man of the pope and on this basis number two in the Church, supplanting the secretary of state who would thus become the keystone of the curia's workings and those of papal diplomacy but not those of the Synodal government; or the secretary of state himself will become officially recognised as the secretary of the Synod. In this latter case the secretary of state would add a third function to those that are already his from his authority over the secretariat of state and from the influence he exercises as prefect of the Council for the Public Business of the Church over the papal diplomatic corps. This number two would thus arrogate to himself an importance unparallelled in the annals of Church government, at least in a case where a pope is ill or overtired or technically poorly prepared for the government of the universal Church.

Such a centralisation of power would certainly be within the logic of developments under Paul VI who increased the powers of the secretary of state and confided in him the task of awakening collegial life in the Church and assuring the Synod's place, prudently, discreetly and gradually, in that life. But if such an accumulation of power under the pope in the hands of some single man did take place, we may be sure that a conclave would speedily move towards the election of a pope who could restrain such power.

The Lord has given his Church a simple and open principle of government which tempers the monarchical principle (with its risks of autocracy) by collegiality (with its risks of confusion). The relation between these two poles may be articulated in a number of ways and is necessarily always in evolution, for its expression depends on historical conjunctions, on the needs of men and the choices open to them. The crisis of the papacy in the Middle Ages gave a preponderance to the collegial principle, so much so that the first and decisive act of the Council of Constance was to depose three popes in order to put an end to schism while declaring the superiority of council over pope.[13] The excesses of this collegialist victory created a breeding ground for the occasionally shady growth of absolute monarchy since that time. That monarchy reached its most accomplished form under Paul VI, the pope who broke the power of the curia. Thanks to the Council, and to those fundamentally sound structures which Paul VI established, we may perhaps have arrived at a moment of balance which will prove genuinely happy and fruitful.

Translated by Aidon Nichols

Notes

1. With the exception, as we shall see, of the 1969 Synod, which took a more effective hold on its own responsibilities.

2. 'Synod' and 'Council' are interchangeable words, as understood in the Acta of the Second Vatican Council. The Council designates itself as *Sacra Synodus* ('Synodus' being a rare second declension feminine noun). Etymologically, the two terms, one Greek, *synodos*, the other Latin, *concilium*, signify a reunion (the prefix 'syn' or 'con'). 'Synod' means a common road (*hodos*), and 'Council' the call to assembly.

3. *Proceres clericorum,* the grand old men of the clergy.

4. R. Laurentin *Bilan du Concile* (Paris 1966) pp. 332-5. See also the six volumes devoted to the three first Synods: *L'Enjeu du Synode* (Paris 1967); *Le Premier Synode, Histoire et Bilan* (Paris 1968); *Enjeu du Deuxième Synode* (Paris 1969); *Le Synode Permanent* (Paris 1970); *Nouveaux Ministères et Fin du Clergé devant le Troisième Synode* (Paris 1971); *Réorientation de l'Eglise après le Troisième Synode* (Paris 1972); *L'Evangélisation après le Quatrième Synode* (Paris 1975).

5. *Annuario Pontificio* (1978) p. 921. The pope was prefect of the Holy Office until the *Annuario* of 1967, p. 935.

6. IDOC Dossier 67-9, pp. 1-4.

7. The regulating document of the Synod, signed on December 8 1966, was published in *Osservatore Romano* for December 24. It has thirty-seven articles. (DC, January 18 1967, No. 1486, pp. 129-140. See also R. Laurentin *L'enjeu du Synode* pp. 97-104.) At the start of the first session Cardinal Felici presented an explanation of this document under the title *Explicationes circa normas pro- cedendi in coetu generali*: seven articles enumerated in Roman figures. At each Synod modifications to this charter, generally of a happy sort, have been made with a view to the better functioning of the gathering.

8. Facts abound in this area. I have given an account of the most striking in the works cited above under note 4. After a period of hesitation at the 1967 and 1969 Synods it was accepted as sufficient for the word to be passed round that the pope did not want this or that and some project would thus be silenced or some clear-cut majority overthrown. To proceed like this behind the scenes was at least venerable custom; whether it is right or wrong is another matter. An example occurred in 1971; see *Réorientation de l'Eglise* (Paris 1972).

9. I refer here to the title and thesis of E. Goblot's pre-structuralist work *La Barrière et le Niveau*. He defined a two-fold principle of class and caste distinctiveness as lying in a 'barrier' against others and a 'difference of level' as seen from within precluding recruitment to the class.

10. This reform has involved one notable resignation, that of Cardinal Bertoli, as well as a chain of reaction following the departure of the man the pope had appointed to invite the resignation of the cardinals of the old curia (Ottaviani, Pizzardo). It has also presented all the curial departments with the problem of the newly centralised oversight and authority of the pope himself.

11. On the election of Cardinal Seper on October 12 1967 (he headed the list with 140 votes) and his nomination as prefect of the Congregation for the Doctrine of the Faith in January 1968, see R. Laurentin *Le Premier Synode* (Paris 1968) pp. 107-8. In other instances the pope has not responded to the choice of individuals in synodal voting and has acted in a sense contrary to that choice. For example he did not give a cardinal's hat to Mgr. Bernardin who was the sole bishop elected in the first round of votes to the permanent council by the Synod of 1974. In the same way, Mgr. Etchegaray, also elected to this permanent council, as well as being president of the European bishops and of the French episcopal conference, has been passed over in promotions. On the other hand the pope has given a definite helping hand to personalities, sometimes controversial, of the 'éminence grise' variety, notably from the traditional curia.

12. The curial offices have been compared to the ministries of a state government. The congregations (qualified by the adjective 'sacred') are analogous to Ministries proper, the Secretariats (for the Union of Christians, for Non-Christians, for Non-believers) and the Councils or Commissions (for the Laity, for Justice and Peace) to secretaryships of state.

13. Thus the Council of Constance's decree of April 6: *Sancta Synodus, legitime congregata . . . et Ecclesiam catholicam repraesentans, potestates a Christo immediate habet, cui quilibet, cujuscumque status vel dignitatis, etiam si papalis existat, obedire tenetur, in his quae pertinent ad fidem et extirpationem . . . schismatis et reformationem dictae Ecclesiae in capite vet in membris.* P. de Vooght has shown with nuance and precision that this decree of Constance was in fact confirmed by Martin V along with all that had been defined *conciliariter* there despite the pope's aversion for conciliar gatherings. See his *Le Concile et les conciles* (Paris 1960) p. 161.

Juan Sánchez y Sánchez

Episcopal Conferences and the Roman Curia

(a) Collegiality

As I begin to write these lines the Holy Spirit has just given a special gift to his Church: the gift of two popes, John Paul I and John Paul II. It seems clear that the first was there for no other reason than to make way for the second. John Paul II, on whom Christian people have already set such high hopes, would not have existed but for the election and premature death of John Paul I. Such are the ways of providence—and they are almost always disconcerting! 'If the grain of wheat dies . . .' The profound mystery of a pope's destiny!

The remarkable thing about this occurrence, a relatively rare event in history, is that it holds within it a *sign of the times*. We could sum it up in this way:

> an open, simple smile, which, as soon as it begins to shine on the world, is cut off by the pressure of a de-humanising curia[1];
> a second conclave, which appeared to be beset by problems;
> a college of cardinals thrown off its bearings by a 'conflict among brothers'; and, thanks to that,
> a centuries-old tradition happily broken, so making way for a non-Italian pope;
> a pope, John Paul II, who seems to be a 'pope with a difference' (time alone will show *how* different).

Here we have a sign which gives a clear revelation, which should find concrete expression, and bring about some change of course at the higher ecclesiastical levels. I am simply recording the fact—nothing more. However I may perhaps be permitted to draw attention to something which seems highly significant: both popes, in their first public utterances, referred to *collegiality* in a very definite way and in almost identical terms. The time has come—both of them more or less declared—for the term to cease to be a beautiful conciliar theory and be turned into a living reality.[2]

Paul VI, for all his undeniable greatness, was imprecise and hesitant at this point. He did not venture to take great decisions. He undoubtedly believed in collegiality, and made some slight attempts to apply it at the level of both the Roman Congregations and the Episcopal Synod. But at heart he appeared not to be completely convinced. It was as if he did not want to have anything actually to do with it. And he left it for his successors to take the step which he himself, because of his mental outlook, would never have taken.

The foregoing leads us into our subject, at the very heart of which throbs a strict problem of collegiality. For us it is clear that the theological mainstay of episcopal conferences is to be found in the doctrine of collegiality. What is functioning in each conference is a part of the college in communion with its head, and for that reason its decisions can come to have binding force for all its members, when the legal requirements are met. To affirm that the idea of collegiality 'non suscipit magis vel minus', that either the college is involved *as a whole* or it is not involved at all, is to affirm too much, which amounts to proving nothing. That, indeed, could be *one kind* of collegiality: full, or first grade, collegiality. But it cannot be the only kind.[3] For we accept, along with the majority of theologians and canonists, that there is a less full collegiality, a second grade collegiality as it were, which is to be seen in a group of bishops met in an episcopal conference in full communion with the pope. If we were to say that none but full collegiality exists, then, as things stand, it would be operative in only two circumstances: in an Ecumenical Council, approved or accepted as such by Peter's successor, and in collegial action exercised by the bishops scattered throughout the world in union with the pope, on condition that the head of the college called them to collegial action, or at least approved or freely accepted their united action.[4] This latter circumstance has never arisen, so far as we know. The Ecumenical Council happens so infrequently, as history shows, that if the exercise of collegiality were reduced simply to that, it would get completely rusted up for want of use. There must necessarily be other kinds of collegiality if we do not want to affirm that it can only be exercised at intervals of centuries.

(b) 'Roman curia'

We have been given the task of writing about episcopal conferences and their relations with the *Roman curia*. We must take this latter expression in a restrictive sense. If we were to extend it to cover the Holy See as a whole, along the lines suggested by canon 7 of the Code of Canon Law, we would not have space even to enumerate the large number of questions—all of them interesting—to which the subject gives rise. Besides, many of them are touched upon in this same issue of *Concilium*.

After these general observations, which seemed necessary, we can now turn our attention to the subject.

The pope acts normally through his curia. He has it because he needs it. Since he cannot attend personally to the large number of matters that come to him, then, in accordance with some very detailed legislation set out principally in the Apostolic Constitution *Regimini Ecclesiae Universae,* he regularly delegates the greater part of his powers to the Roman curia which then acts and decides in his name and on his behalf.

A CHANGING SITUATION

It is by no means easy today to speak of the relations between the Roman curia and episcopal conferences. Before such conferences had a legally defined existence, the commonest relationship, almost the only one (since provincial or plenary councils were hardly ever held), was that of the bishop with the pope, normally through his curia. In general, this relationship presented no special problems. It proceeded peacefully along the lines laid down in the Code and in accordance with the regular 'praxis', which had hardened into custom. Problems arose as a result of the Second Vatican Council, and were caused by the collegial activity of the conferences. This is certainly a new development, with its own special features. And in our judgment it is a mistake to continue attempting to fit such new and different realities into the old moulds in use before the Council.

IS THE RELATION BETWEEN CURIA AND CONFERENCES ONE OF CONFLICT?

We must make a distinction. Theoretically, from the point of view of the papal office which prevails today, there is no conflict. So long as things are looked at only *from above,* which is what is happening, no conflict exists. For the curia continues to be the faithful instrument of the pope, helping him to govern the universal Church, and he can therefore remit to it whatever matters he chooses, not excluding those relating to episcopal conferences themselves. In fact this is what is set out in No. 50 of *Regimini Ecclesiae Universae*: 'Congregationis pro Episcopis est . . . ea perpendere quae ad Coetus Episcoporum seu Conferentias attinet'.

But if we look at things from the point of view of collegiality, from the standpoint of the college itself, we find that the situation prevailing at present lends itself to confusion and may lead to conflicts.

Episcopal conferences are playing an increasingly important part in the study and solution of the socio-religious and pastoral problems of nations. It was to this end that the Council gave them its approval. This kind of activity follows predominantly a practical line, and at times includes a magisterial function. It is not unusual for it to result in legislative measures on a number of issues. All these are aspects of a *collegial* activity which previously did not take place.

We consider, on the basis of several clear texts of Vatican II, that it is necessary for this collegial action of a country's hierarchy to be linked up with the principle which informs the whole college.[5] But this principle is the head of the college. It is the pope himself, and not the curia, which is something very different. Many voices raised in the Council insisted that the college is above the curia, and not the reverse. The curia indeed was viewed with some misgiving. It is true that the voices referred to the complete college, with its head. It is also true that the conferences are not the college. But they are part of it, and they carry out a collegial action which is not only important but even, in a way, irreplaceable for the nation in which they act. Therefore they imply a considerable change as compared with the previous situation, by the express wish of the Council.

Because of all this it would have seemed fitting that attempts should be made in Rome to seek a new solution to the problem of relating episcopal conferences to the Pontiff. And the easy way out—of placing their activity under the authority of the Congregation of Bishops, or else distributing the matters sent forward by them among the various Congregations in accordance with their respective responsibilities—should have been avoided. Episcopal conferences, which are founded on the principle of collegiality, remain undervalued.

THE EXAMPLE OF THE SYNOD OF BISHOPS

What Pope Paul VI did with the Episcopal Synod is instructive. In its structure the Synod is composed in the main of representatives from episcopal conferences all over the world. Pope Paul did not want to link it with the Roman curia. Instead he by-passed the curia and brought the Synod into direct relationship with himself through its secretariat. This in spite of the fact that the presidents or prefects of the Roman departments are part of the Synod. He sought in this way to preserve the priority of the Episcopal College when it functions in union with its head, a priority recognised in the Church today. It is true that the bishops of the Synod are not the College. They cannot even claim to be official representatives of it. It is also true that as things stand at present, and unless the pope decides otherwise, the Synod is not the official organ by which collegiality is expressed.[6] Nevertheless, to avoid the difficulties which might have resulted from linking the Synod with the curia, the pope chose not to link them, and his decision met with general approval.

We believe that something similar should happen with the episcopal conferences. In them collegial activity takes place—the collegial activity of a greater or smaller proportion of the members of the college. The doctrinal basis for such activity, as we have already indicated, is in the very collegiality approved by the Council, and the principle which informs it is the Roman Pontiff as head of the College. It is directly with him, then, and not with his curia, that the activity of the conferences should be linked. As is the case with the Synod.

PRINCIPLES ON WHICH A SOLUTION MAY BE BASED

The basic problem which underlies all that we have been discussing is strictly theological, though inevitably it has juridical consequences. Various solutions have been sought for the juridical problems, though from widely divergent viewpoints. Let us look at some of them:

(a) Participation of the bishops in the organisms of the curia

This is the solution proposed by Paul VI in *Regimini*. Seven bishops, as a general rule, chosen from all over the world, should be present in Rome once a year for the general meeting of the Congregation to which they have been assigned. At first this seemed a significant development. The Roman Congregations were, by definition, exclusively colleges of cardinals. That some diocesan bishops should begin to belong to them 'iure proprio, tamquam membra stricte dicta' was canonically incongruous. But Paul VI wanted it that way, and his will prevailed.

With the passing of the years (it is now twelve years since *Regimini* appeared), it has become apparent that the introduction of these appointments has contributed very little to a more active and effective presence of the episcopal college and the conferences in the Roman curia. These bishops make their way to Rome once a year for a very specific piece of business, make their appearance in the plenary sessions, then take their leave . . . until the following year. They are not even consulted about the drawing up of the agenda for the meetings. In effect they find everything already cut and dried. Their contribution is minimal, and no-one supposes today that either the episcopal college or the conferences are represented in this way, even though this was the intention of such appointments.

On various occasions, more recently, the problem has been debated again. And the desire has been expressed for the number of diocesan bishops in the Roman curia to be increased. This has been seen as a necessary consequence of the responsibility of the bishops for the life and work of the Church, as it is defined in the teaching of the Council. This was what various groups of synodal fathers demanded in the extra-ordinary assembly of 1969, which dealt directly with the question. But we do not know how far such a multiplication of diocesan bishops would be representative, or, above all, how far it could be effective, while the internal working of the congregations continues as it is at present. Its results must be in doubt so long as the prefects maintain their almost all-embracing power, and so long as the bishops are not in a position to follow more closely the day-to-day and detailed progress of the depart-ments.

(b) Closer collaboration between the Roman Pontiff and the conferences

This is another of the solutions which have been put forward as necess-ary consequences of the doctrine of collegiality. On the one hand it would be expected that the pope should consult the episcopal conferences about all matters of major importance concerning the universal government of the Church. On the other hand, the episcopal conferences would have to be happy to submit all their actions for the pope's approval. Doubtless an effective principle, but an inadequate one.

(c) Above the curia

If the Roman congregations were to abide faithfully by the principles governing notification and approval which are actually in force, both those laid down in the Code (c. 244) and those in *Regimini* (Nos. 12 and 136), then it would be to the highest authority, that of the pope, that the most delicate matters of the conferences were referred. These principles require the congregations to bring to the notice of the Pontiff any *serious* or *extraordinary* matter before taking any decision over it. However, experience unhappily shows that the congregations do not always consult the pope about their most serious decisions, in spite of the constitutional obligation to do so.[7] And so long as the situation remains unchanged they will feel obliged to intervene whenever questions of their competence are at issue. From their point of view this may be legitimate, but it is not particularly appreciated by the conferences, because they feel, rightly, that different levels of decision-making are involved. The curia is below the college, and they, the conferences, are part of the college.

(d) A central organism

So that there might be more direct and more regular co-operation between the conferences and the pope, there are many who would like the conferences to have a central organism in Rome to represent them and to follow developments closely. This desire seems to us logical. The conferences are becoming constantly more active, particularly in the magisterial and legislative fields. With the multiplication of these various documents throughout the world—and they are already numbered in hundreds—we are heading for a state of confusion which could be quite overwhelming, if the development of this activity is not closely watched with a view to its being co-ordinated and related to the parallel activity of the Holy See. Because there are so many conferences, and because the circumstances and places in which they act are so diverse, because, too, their members have been chosen in different ways,[8] and because the questions call for differences in approach, it could happen that identical problems received contradictory solutions. Hence the necessity, in our judgment, for a central organism which could follow developments and avoid possible deviations—a body with which the episcopal conferences would have to be in direct relation. Pluralism is healthy, so long as it does not affect the essentials. A state of confusion is always harmful, even when it only touches the inessentials.

(e) What sort of a body could this be?

1. *The Congregation of Bishops*—one among the Roman congregations? Although we would not deny its competence, if conferred by the pope (and in fact today it possesses such competence), we do not think that either this or any other congregation is the most appropriate body for this mission of liaison with organs which, in greater or lesser degree, correspond to the episcopal college. The latter, regardless of the level at which it is considered, is, as we have said repeatedly, above the curia in theory. And it must also be above the curia in practice.

2. *The Secretariat of the Synod?* The secretariat as it is and as it operates today would not be the ideal body for this mission either. Its present function bears no relation to the episcopal conferences. Given a very different conception of the Roman curia and the Synod, this secretariat could be the most appropriate body for the purpose we are considering. At present it is not. Apart from which, as is well known, in all the sessions of the Synod which have been held to date, its work has been completely subjected to the most rigid controls and to the authoritarian directives of the Secretariat of State—as is generally rumoured among the synodal fathers themselves. This naturally gives rise to suspicion and creates mistrust among the members of the episcopal college.

3. *A new organism?* Perhaps it would not be necessary. But instead a radical change in the structuring of the Roman curia, in fidelity to the doctrine of the Second Vatican Council.

We have expressed elsewhere[9] serious reservations about the reform of the Roman curia carried out by Paul VI. We do not deny that in many aspects it represented a notable advance and that it achieved remarkable results which no-one expected. But we can never understand why the reform should have been carried out without changing the basic structure laid down by Sixtus V in the sixteenth century. This basic structure was conceived in the intellectual and socio-religious climate of 1588, when the pope was ruler of vast territories, when the pontifical court left a great deal to be desired, when the college of cardinals was riddled with defects, when (and this is the most serious) the body of bishops counted for nothing, because the bishops had little connection with the Roman See in consequence of a system of royal appointment which led to their being linked up with the prince rather than the pope. How is it possible that such a structure should be considered capable of supporting a reform which is put into effect following a Council which has given enormous importance to the episcopate in the Church? How is it possible that so little account should be taken of the episcopate?[10]

The papacy is a permanent function of the life of the Church. It has its curia. Is not the episcopal college, with its head, also a permanent function? It certainly is if we take into account the texts of Vatican II. And if it is a permanent function it is logical that it also should have its curia. But this does not mean that we should think of two curias. The pope and the bishops form a single college. The normal thing would be for this college as such—pope and bishops—to have a single curia which would aid them both—pope and college—in the one mission which has been entrusted to them: the government of the universal Church. If both together—pope and college—are vested with supreme power in the Church, if both hold at the highest level universal responsibility for its life and work, then it will be necessary for the curia to serve both equally—along with such organisms as may be considered effective (perhaps with the same ones it has now). But residential bishops would have to be in the forefront, preferably those engaged in the pastoral office, transferred to Rome to perform these duties temporarily.

A curia set up over the college of cardinals is *today* an anachronism. As is the college of cardinals itself. It is a 'double' which may have an explanation historically but which at the present time does not make sense and which seems to demand a return to authentic unity, to the *only* college which Christ founded and gave to his Church under the supreme pastor and indisputable head, the pope.

4. *New criteria for a new restructuring of the curia*

The matter of primary importance, in our judgment, would be to pay the most careful attention to the body of specialists in each department, which should be composed of experts, whether clergy or laymen, from all over the world. It would be necessary then carefully to select the most gifted from among them and place them in positions of responsibility, including the post of secretary, which would not then be held by a bishop. With a staff prepared and given responsibility in this way the departments would function of their own accord with whatever powers the pope and the college might choose to give them. There would be no craving for more attractive posts, and no anxiety or haste to attain them (because they would have disappeared). The figure of an indispensable president or prefect would not need to be so much part of the department. It would suffice to place at its head a residential bishop with enough ability to take charge of its operation—one who could bring his pastoral and practical experience to bear on the plans which the staff of the department would work out in detail under his direction. He would hold office for three years, but would not relinquish his diocese completely. He would leave in charge of it an auxiliary bishop with special powers, who would only need to consult the diocesan bishop about the most serious matters. The assembly of the Synod, which now takes place regularly every three years, could be the occasion for making changes in these appointments. The pope would then have the opportunity of exchanging views with bishops from all over the world, and, in consultation with them, of putting in charge of the departments those members of the episcopal college who were most suitable in the judgment of all, and who would then form a kind of *permanent Synod* by the side of the Pontiff.

In this possible solution, very summarily described, the conferences would link up with the curia through their own representatives, and, above all, through the Synod and its permanent secretariat. This would become 'ipso facto' the central organism of the whole curia, and would acquire a position of primacy, as the organ of co-operation and union of the world-wide episcopate within itself and with its head. It would make for the effective government of the whole Church through a common curia.

Translated by G. W. S. Knowles

Notes

1. Let us be quite clear. This interpretation of events is part of the *sign*. We are not going to analyse it, but it spreads everywhere like an oil-slick. The public accepts it, believes it and is filled with astonishment—while at the same time reacting against the curia.

2. Following the directions we have been given, we are not going to overload our statements with footnotes. The passages to which we refer can be easily found in the early addresses of both popes. A number of cardinals also made frequent and significant declarations on this subject, as if there were a general desire among them for the future pope to tackle this problem.

3. We have in mind an important book on this whole question published by the Faculty of Canon Law of the Pontifical University of Salamanca: *Las Conferencias Episcopales Hoy* (Salamanca 1977).

4. *Lumen Gentium,* 22.

5. *Lumen Gentium,* 22, 2; 23, 2; 27, 1; nota expl. praev. 3; *Christus Dominus,* 8 (a), etc.

6. The *supremacy* of the episcopal college, including, by implication, its head, is today explicitly recognised by the Church: 'Ordo autem Episcoporum . . . subiectum *quoque* supremae ac plenae potestatis in universam Ecclesiam exsistit' (*Lumen Gentium,* 22). The problem is the *intentional ambiguity* of the constitutional texts concerning the episcopal Synod, which can be interpreted in two completely conflicting ways: (a) the *collegial* way: 'utpote totius catholici Episcopatus partes agens' (*Christus Dominus,* 5). On the basis of this text the Synod would indeed be the official representative of the whole Catholic episcopate (understood to include the pope who is its head), and it would also be the official organ of expression of the College. But there exists also the other interpretation which we might call: (b) the *papal* way: 'Supremo Ecclesiae Pastori validiorem praestant adiutricem operam' (*ibid.*). According to this version the Synod is neither the College nor its representative (because it is explicitly separated from its head), nor is it its official organ of expression. In his *Apostolica Sollicitudo,* by which the Synod is created and regulated, Paul VI follows literally the *papal* interpretation. But we are convinced that a different pope, to whom the collegial version might be more congenial, could change the direction of the Synod, and for the good of the Church we trust that such a pope will not be long in arriving.

7. There occurred in 1972 in connection with the Spanish Episcopal Conference, a very strange case, brought about by the Congregation of Clergy. The latter, surprised in its good faith by persons connected with the department (whose faith, it seems was not so good), addressed directly to the main organisms of the conference a document which was in a certain sense condemnatory. When the president of the conference had recourse to the Secretariat of State to seek certain clarifications it was revealed that, despite the extreme seriousness of the matter, everything had remained at the level of the congregation itself, and superior organisms, including the pope himself, knew nothing at all of it. (Religious reviews of the period may be consulted, e.g., *Vida Nueva,* Nos. 824-825, for March 18/25 1972—a double number concerned almost entirely with this problem—and *Iglesia Viva,* No. 38 (1972) pp. 109-248.)

8. The comparison naturally arises between an episcopate chosen from a large body of well-trained clergy and an episcopate to which certain candidates are nominated . . . because there are no others. It is a complex problem, difficult to solve, and producing serious consequences. The mission of the nuncios carries, in this sense, enormous responsibility. For these nominations there should be a more decisive involvement on the part of the conferences themselves, since they are more familiar with particular situations. In certain cases and specific countries the unfortunate actions of a nuncio in nominating bishops will be seen in history as paralysing effective apostolic action.

9. See 'La constitution apostolique *Regimini ecclesiae universae* six ans après' in *l'Année Canonique XX* (1976) pp. 41-44.

10. We believe that any reform which is to be carried through in the Church must be along the lines of open renewal in the Council. For that reason we are not in complete agreement with something which now seems irremediable: the promulgation of the *revised* Code of Canon Law of 1917. It is more than evident to us that the doctrinal, and in some ways the constitutional, content of Vatican II demands not merely a *revised* Code but a completely new one. It has to be borne in mind that when, on March 28 1963, John XXIII appointed the pontifical commission for the revision of the Code, the Council had only just begun its work. The Code was based on a pre-conciliar theology. The constitutions and decrees of Vatican II, above all the *Lumen Gentium,* open up completely new paths, unknown to the older theology. The attempt to harmonise this new theology with a great part of the provisions of a Code which is merely *revised* will be very difficult, perhaps impossible. In such circumstances it would not be surprising if the 'new' Code were to be born without the conditions necessary for survival and, if not already dead, at least in its death throes, unless suitable remedies can be applied.

Antonio Vitale

The Roman Curia as an International Centre of Collaboration and Charity

1. PASTORAL SERVICE OR MONARCHICAL IDEOLOGY?

THE ROMAN curia comprises those departments, tribunals and offices 'which co-operate in the general government of the Catholic Church'.[1]

The ecclesiological justification for the curia resides, therefore in this function of co-operating in the 'general pastoral government': a function which derives from 'the constitutional requirements of the apostolic ministry', and of which the concrete expression must be 'fraternal and directed towards the good of the Church as a whole'.[2] Consequently it is clear that it is the way in which this 'general pastoral government' is understood which determines the disposition of the Roman curia. To say, in fact that 'the present disposition of the curia itself is the historical and political result of the progressive assertion of the monarchical ideology at the highest levels of the Church',[3] is tantamount to calling in question, at least in its contingent mode of operation, precisely this 'papal monarchy'.

It can therefore be agreed that demands for the transformation of the Roman curia are the result of pressures emerging from various ecclesiological sources to see what is and should be the papal service within the context of the Church.

2. THE 1967 REFORM: CAUTIOUS AND UNSUCCESSFUL

It seems strange that one should be recording these demands for change within the Roman curia, given that only a little more than ten years have passed since Pope Paul VI decreed the reform of that same curia, with the constitution *Regimini Ecclesiae Universalis* of August 15 1967.[4]

The reform of Paul VI was substantially inspired by three principal criteria:

(a) Aggiornamento

The name of the Congregation of the Holy Office has been modified, becoming the Congregation for the Doctrine of the Faith, and in the cases that come before it the right of defence has been introduced; in addition to Latin, use may be made of the modern language most familiar to the individual involved; outdated institutions and functions have been suppressed; new bodies have been created.

(b) Reorganisation

There has been a desire on the one hand, to ensure that the initiatives of the pope are not too restricted by the bureaucratic machine (hence it has been established that curial functions cease automatically at the death of the pontiff), and on the other to encourage communication both between departments and between the departments and the bishops (to which end some diocesan bishops have been introduced as members of the sacred congregations).

(c) Emphasis on the characteristic of service

The risk of ecclesiatical careerism has been avoided through the adoption of the rule according to which appointment to the higher offices cannot be for more than five years.[5]

In spite of all this, concrete experience has demonstrated just how unsuccessful such cautious reform is, for it manages, in the end, to make the situation worse at the very moment when, in order to protect the pope from the restrictions and entanglements of the bureaucratic machine, it emphasised the role of bodies, like the Secretariat of State, which have revealed a marked tendency towards authoritarian centralism.[6] And that is why, in spite of the 1967 reform, the demands for changes in the Roman curia consonant with the developments in ecclesiology stimulated by Vatican II, remain valid and relevant.

3. CENTRE OF UNIVERSAL COMMUNION

In an ecumenical perspective, the growing insistence on the need for a visible centre of unity for the universal Church is closely bound up with another need, an indispensable presupposition of the first: that the papacy should act as the dynamic centre of initiative, presenting itself as an evangelical symbol and as the source of universal values.

In the light of this new role of papal service, the present structure of the Roman curia will eventually be revealed as an inhibiting element. It is generally admitted, for example, that in his attempts to interpret this new role, Pope John XXIII came up against the stolid resistance of the complex bureaucratic machine of the curia. A Roman curia, therefore, that is going to function usefully within the framework of the new service which can and should be rendered by the Roman Church, will necessarily have to submit to having its present complicated structure reorganised in favour of the least structure possible—a structure that is modest and flexible, and does not subject its contact with the other churches to an excess of filtering processes and intermediaries.

4. AUTONOMY OF THE LOCAL CHURCHES

A second line of development is constituted by right appreciation of the local churches—an appreciation which signifies in concrete terms recognition of autonomy and the right to self-government. Alongside this type of recognition stands the Roman curia, which still centralises a considerable number of functions, the exercise of which is characterised, in addition, by that 'curial style'. This, incredibly enough, given that it appertains to an executive body, is raised to the status of a subsidiary source of law (can. 20 of the Code of Canon Law), and, refined as it is by a centuries-old practice and dictated by the instinct for conservation characteristic of every centre of power, it is shrouded in an atmosphere of suspicion and mistrust and authoritarianism, thus restricting the experimentation and research which could make the Church an effective interpreter of those religious needs which are connected with the territories and milieux in which she finds herself.

The local churches could well be entrusted—with obvious additional advantages from the economic and financial point of view—with functions related to the appointment of bishops, the discipline of marriage and the resolution of matrimonial cases, the discipline of the clergy, liturgy and pastoral work, and so on.

Against the possibility that the local churches might themselves become bureaucratised[7] should be set the tolerable counterweight not only of an organisation that is closer to, and therefore more adapted to the particular needs involved and the consequent efficiency of those trying to meet them, but also of a corresponding debureaucratisation of the Roman curia, which would in every way be advantageous to the exercise of those functions which best express the new role which the papal service must fulfil.

5. CENTRE OF CHARITY

A third line of development follows from the implications of the concept of the Church as community and as servant.

Looking through the *Acta* dating from the period of preparation for the second Vatican Council, one can see that among the proposals put forward by the Italian bishops there was one to the effect that the Roman congregations should be involved in works of assistance; that Cardinal Garrone, in the proposals sent to Rome on August 30 1959, expressed the hope that the Roman curia might be organised in such a way as to be a 'sign' and a 'cause' of unity; that from many sides came the request that the curia, far from restricting itself to a negative controlling function, should regard it as its duty to serve and assist the local churches.

There were, in addition, more concrete proposals, such as that a single centre should be established to co-ordinate all charitable activities, perhaps through the creation of a new congregation (Bishop Mazzocco of Adria), or an organisation for the management of financial resources and their redistribution on a rational basis, or else a social security service for priests throughout the world.

6. SERVICE THROUGH COLLABORATION AND SOLIDARITY

As far as the possibility of expressing these requirements in terms of suitable structures and institutions is concerned, the question seemed to become easier from the moment when Pope John Paul II, in his inaugural discourse,[8] not only emphasised in passing 'the bond of collegiality which links the bishops closely to the successor of Peter and to each other', but also predicted the institutional expression of the need for collegiality through 'the appropriate development of those bodies, sometimes new, sometimes updated, which can secure a better union of heart, will and initiative in building up the body of Christ, which is the Church'.

Consequently, one might propose in the first place, a redefinition of the functions of the Roman curia, which should be concerned with anything connected with the bond of union between the churches—should, that is, turn its attention to problems which affect several churches, transcending national and continental boundaries, or else to disputes between churches, or to nominations for central offices like that of president of a regional or continental conference of bishops, for which the *placet* of the pope, as guarantor of communion, could be sought.

Secondly, the Roman curia should become a centre of initiative and inspiration. In the theological field, instead of operating a machine designed to hand down judgments against doctrines held to be erroneous, and therefore implicitly to discouraging freedom of thought and research, it should be organised in such a way as to encourage research, promote reflection and study and facilitate the task of scholars by providing them with the tools they need.

Thirdly, taking up suggestions already made twenty years ago by the Lombardi Fathers, the curia should be so organised as to provide a general and regularly updated assessment of the needs of the Catholic Church, and so to rationalise the deployment of forces—including distribution of priests, maximum use of the human talent available to the Church, exchange of experience, circulation of financial assets—on a world-wide basis. It should not, in fact, be forgotten, that many churches are *poor* in the matter of personnel, resources, inspiration and freedom. So this function would appear to be all the more necessary, in that there is a danger today that *weak* churches will also be *alienated,* as a result of the inevitable relationship of dependence they establish with the richer, more powerful churches which undoubtedly help them, but which also make them feel their cultural, economic and political influence.

Fourthly, and precisely in view of this service of collaboration and solidarity, many congregations should be radically transformed in so far as their role is concerned: for example, the Sacred Congregation for the Evangelisation of Peoples should stop acting as the Church's central department for evangelisation and take on instead the task of inter-ecclesial assistance—it should serve, that is, as a meeting place, where the local churches, young and old, can examine the problems that arise from their mutual service.

Finally, those organisations of more recent foundation which have been added to the number of the traditional Roman curial departments, should be developed—though at the same time rescued from the centralising and authoritarian logic in which they at present run the risk of becoming enmeshed—in order to find an answer to the real problems which trouble Christianity scattered throughout the world; and above all, among these, the *Cor Unum,* which acts as principal co-ordinating body for Catholic charitable and aid agencies, and which would seem, for this reason, to epitomise the spirit and the corresponding organisational structure which one looks for in the Roman curia as a whole.

Translated by Sarah Fawcett

Notes

1. Paul VI, *Discourse* of February 22 1975, in *Acta Apostolicae Sedis* 1975, p. 196.

2. Paul VI, *loc. cit.*

3. G. Alberigo 'Towards a Renewed Papacy at the Service of the Church' in *Concilium* 8, 1975.

4. On February 22 1968, the general regulations, which had been provided for by the constitution itself, were approved. It should be recalled that prior to the constitution *Regimini Ecclesiae Universalis,* the organisation of the Roman curia was based on the constitution *Sapienti Consilio,* which was approved by Pope Pius X on June 29 1908, the contents of which had been absorbed into the *Codex Iuris Canonici.* See M. Petrocelli *Diritto Canonico* (Naples 1976) pp. 202 ff.

5. See in this connection J. P. Manigne 'La réforme de la curie: patience et fermeté' in *Informations Catholiques Internationales* 530 (September 1978) pp. 31 ff.

6. See G. Zizola *Quale Papa?* (Rome 1977).

7. See Hans Urs von Balthasar *Le Complexe Anti-Romain. Essai sur les Structures Ecclésiales* (Paris 1976) pp. 40 ff.

8. *Osservatore Romano* October 18 1978, p. 3; *The Tablet* October 28 1978, p. 1049.

Contributors

GIUSEPPE ALBERIGO was born in Varese in 1926. Since 1967 he has lectured on Church History at the faculty of Political Studies at Bologna University. He is also Secretary of the Institute of Religious Studies in Bologna, and a member of the *Concilium* international committee. His publications include books on the Council of Trent, the development of the concept of power in the Church, collegiality, and Pope John XXIII, and he is currently working on a study of conciliarism in the fifteenth and sixteenth centuries.

JOSÉ DAMMERT BELLIDO was born in Lima (Peru) in 1917. He was awarded the degree of Doctor in Jurisprudence by the University of Pavia (Italy), and served as Professor of Law in the Catholic University of Lima until his appointment as Auxiliary Bishop of Lima. Since 1962 he has been Bishop of Cajamarca. He is a consultant of the Pontifical Commission for the revision of Canon Law, and has written articles on legal, historical and pastoral subjects for ecclesiastical reviews published in Lima and in Spain.

EMMA CAVALLARO was born in 1936. She is married and lives in Rome, where she is at present chief press officer and publications editor for Azione Cattolica Italiana (ACI). She has been and still is involved in the work of a number of women's organisations on a European and a world scale. She is currently a member of the organising committee of the Office Catholiques d'Information sur les Problèmes Européens (OCIPE). She contributes regularly on matters concerning women and on family problems to the Italian Catholic daily *Avvenire,* as well as to numerous journals.

LAMBERTO DE ECHEVERRÍA was born in 1918 in Vitoria (Spanish-Basque region) and ordained priest in 1941. He lectures in both Civil and Pontifical Universities. He also has wide pastoral experience, and established and manages *Incunable*—a newspaper for Priests. He is founding Director of the Pastoral Institute of Salamanca. He is a frequent contributor to the *Revista española de Derecho canónico*. His latest book is *Oratoria universitaria salmantina*—a study of academic and religious oratory throughout the 750-year history of the University of Salamanca.

NORBERT GREINACHER was born in 1931 in Freiburg in Breisgau, and ordained priest in 1956. He is professor of pastoral theology at the University of Tübingen and has written widely on the relation of the Church to society. His publications include *Die Kirche in der städtischen Gesellschaft* (Mainz 1966, with H. Risse); *Regionalplanung in der Kirche* (Mainz 1965); *Einführung in die Praktische Theologie* (Munich 1976, with R. Zerfass); *Vor einem neuen politischen Katholizismus?* (Frankfurt 1978, with F. Klostermann).

ZENON GROCHOLEWSKI was born in 1939 in Brodki (Poland). Ordained in 1963 he worked in a parish in Roznan (Poland). In 1972 he obtained a degree in Canon Law at the Gregorian Pontifical University in Rome, and in 1974 he obtained his diploma as Lawyer of the Sacred Rota. At present he is chancellor of the Apostolic Signatura and teaches canonical jurisprudence at the Gregorian University. He has published *De exclusione indissolubilitatis ex consensu matrimoniali eiusque probatione* (Naples 1973, with I. Gordon); *Documenta recentiora circa rem matrimonialem et processualem* (Rome 1977); and various articles in journals of canon law.

JAN HEIJKE was born in Amsterdam in 1927. He now teaches missiology at the Catholic University of Nijmegen. In addition to articles in such journals as *Bijdragen, Spiritus, Kosmos en Oekumene, Geist und Leben, Wereld en Zending, Tijdschrift voor Theologie* and *Speling,* he has also published *The Image of God according to St Augustine (De Trinitate Excepted)* (Notre Dame 1956); *An Ecumenical Light: Taizé* (Pittsburgh 1967); *The Bible on Faith* (London 1966).

RENÉ LAURENTIN was born in 1917 at Tours and was ordained priest in 1967. He holds a chair of theology at the University of Angers and has also taught in universities in Canada, the United States and Latin America. A consultative adviser to the preparatory theological Commission of the Second Vatican Council, he later became a Council *peritus.* Religious editor of *Le Figaro,* he is also vice-president of the French Society for Marian Studies and is involved in pastoral ministry near Paris. His numerous writings, many of which touch on the themes of Mariology and of the Second Vatican Council, include *Développement et salut, Nouveaux Ministères et fin du clergé: Réorientation de l'Eglise après le troisième Synode; Lourdes, Documents authentiques; Dieu est-il mort? Crise et promesse d'Eglise aux U.S.A.; Pentecôtisme chez les Catholiques.* The Abbé Laurentin also edits the Mariological section of the *Revue des Sciences Philosophiques et Théologiques.*

JOSEPH LÉCUYER, born in Kerfourn (France), 1912, joined the Holy Ghost Fathers in 1930, obtained his doctorate in philosophy and theology, and lectures at the Gregorianum and at S. Anselmo. Among other works he published *Études sur la collégialité épiscopale* (Lyon 1964).

GREGORIO DELGADO DEL RIO was born in 1940 at Los Villares (Soria). At present he is Professor of Ecclesiastical Organisation in the Faculty of Canon Law in the University of Navarre. He is a member of the *Family Division* of the CERSIP. His many publications include the following: *Deconcentracion organica y potestad vicaria* (Pamplona 1971); *El gobierno central de la Iglesia* (Pamplona 1973); *Error y matrimonio canonico* (Pamplona 1975); *Los obispos auxiliares* (Pamplona 1979).

JUAN SÁNCHEZ Y SÁNCHEZ was born at Macotera in the province of Salamanca (Spain) in 1919. He was ordained priest in 1942. He spent twelve years in Rome, and during this time was in daily contact with the Roman curia. He is a doctor in Canon Law and is at present Dean of the Faculty of Canon Law in the Pontifical University of Salamanca. His publications include: *Pablo VI y la reforma de la curia romana* (Salamanca 1967) and *El vicario episcopal* (Salamanca 1971).

HANSJAKOB STEHLE was born in 1927 and studied history, philosophy and international law in Germany and Italy. He is a journalist who has worked as Warsaw and Berlin correspondent for the *Franfurte Allgemeine Zeitung,* as a regular contributor to *Zeit* and as East and South-eastern European correspondent of West German and North German Radio, whose Rome correspondent he has been since 1970. His publications include *The Independent Satellite. Society and Politics in Poland* (New York/London 1965) and *Die Ostpolitik des Vatikans 1917-1975* (Munich/Zurich 1975).

ANTONIO VITALE was born in Salerno in 1936. He has taught ecclesiastical law in the universities of Bologna and Naples, and is at present ordinary professor of ecclesiastical law at the University of Salerno. Prominent among his less recent works are *L'ufficio ecclesiastico* (Naples 1965) and *Sacramenti e diritto* (Rome/Freiburg 1967); and among the more recent, *Lezioni di diritto ecclesiatico* (Naples 1974), *Il diritto ecclesiastico* (Milan 1978) and *Ordinamento giuridico e fenomeno religioso* (Milan 1979).

GIANCARLO ZIZOLA was born in 1936 in the province of Treviso (Italy). He is a journalist and editor of the Department of Religious Information in the Milan daily 'Il Giorno'. He is one of the founders and secretary of the Centro Culturale per l'Informazione Religiosa, a centre in Rome where scholars and journalists interested in contemporary religious affairs can meet. His publications include *Il sinodo dei vescovi* (Turin 1968); *La riforma del Sant'Offizio* (Turin 1969); *l'Utopia di papa Giovanni* (Assissi 1973; translated into five languages); *Quale papa?* (Rome 1977).